Ating Kalagayan

The Social and Economic Profile of U.S. Filipinos

Peter Chua

in conjunction with the
National Bulosan Center and the
National Alliance for Filipino Concerns
2009

Acknowledgement
The National Bulosan Center is grateful to many organizations and individuals for their advice and assistance in the development of *Ating Kalagayan*. The responsibility for creating and producing it, however, rests entirely with the author. Consultant, artwork, and photo credits are given to the National Alliance for Filipino Concerns Council members, Filipino Community Support of Silicon Valley members, Migrante International, Bulatlat.com, Rhonda Ramino, Michael Luat, Godfrey Ramos, Dr. Robyn Rodriguez, Valerie Francisco, Apollo Victoria, Jonna Baldres, and many others.

The **National Alliance for Filipino Concerns** (NAFCON) is an alliance of U.S. organizations and individuals working to protect and advance the rights and welfare of Filipinos, respond to the basic needs and interests of U.S. Filipinos, promote Filipino heritage, and pursue the call for international justice.

The **National Bulosan Center** serves the needs of grassroots U.S. Filipino organizations and their members, conducts analysis that provides information on the struggles of Filipinos against injustice, and develops resources for their active participation and collective empowerment.

Peter Chua, Ph.D. is associate professor of sociology at San José State University, San José, CA, USA. He has published numerous scholarly studies, conducted first-hand research in India, the Philippines, and Thailand, and presented his research in Spain, Australia, South Africa, and the USA.

National Bulosan Center
4021 69th St, Suite A
Woodside, NY 11377 USA

Contents

Figures

Tables

Foreword

It is good for us to strengthen our commitment to the rights and welfare of Filipinos in the United States of America as well as to our kababayan whom we have left behind in the Philippines by studying and reflecting on *Ating Kalagayan* and

Rev. Benjamin E. Alforque, MSC, VF, President, National Alliance for Filipino Concerns

similar writings. In doing so, we equally commit our deepest sense of multiracial and international solidarity, not only with Filipinos in the Philippines and other U.S. ethnic communities, but with all the peoples of the world, for the cause of human rights and people's welfare.

Ating Kalagayan presents the untold portrait of individuals and groups in the U.S. Filipino community and reflects on our needs and concerns to build our common future. Our goal is to spark a broad and informed discussion on the economic and social conditions of U.S. Filipinos and to aid in organizing and mobilizing efforts to defend our rights and welfare.

We hope *Ating Kalagayan* allows us to address better the worsening economic crisis that is besetting our life in the U.S. and adds to the knowledge on Filipinos globally. We hope that by doing so, we will be guided in our advocacy and campaigns for the cause of human rights and people's welfare, wherever we are, wherever these are violated.

Mabuhay ang mga Pinoy sa Amerika!

Maraming salamat po.

March 2009

Preface

The current and pressing situation of Filipinos in the United States remains often invisible to many. To overcome this invisibility, the National Alliance for Filipino Concerns (NAFCON) commissioned the National Bulosan Center to bring together the most comprehensive demographic data available, conduct specialized tabulations on the data, and document the social issues of various sectors and classes of U.S. Filipinos.

The findings of this commissioned study are presented in this brief yet comprehensive report, which was a collective effort of ordinary people, academic researchers and grassroots local organizers. As a result, this report provides concrete facts and figures on U.S. Filipinos. It gives details on the economic classes of U.S. Filipinos and social groups among them. In addition, it analyzes their particular conditions.

Members of grassroots community-based organizations and other individuals benefit from reading, studying, and discussing this report because it allows them to address better the social and economic concerns of U.S. Filipinos. The report also allows them to arouse, organize, and mobilize U.S. Filipinos more intensely on important issues in the U.S., the Philippines, and other countries.

Improvements for future editions of *Ating Kalagayan* require ongoing local validation, clarification, and elaboration.

1 Introduction

What drives Filipinos to migrate to the United States and other countries worldwide?

Filipinos leave the Philippines due to the worsening conditions of **landlessness, joblessness**, and **economic hardship**, resulting from decades of corrupt politicians, elitist landlords, and greedy big business owners in the Philippines. These conditions in rural agricultural areas and in urban industrial and service centers force Filipinos to leave and migrate to the United States and 190 other countries in search of jobs and better economic opportunities. In addition, businesses and organizations such as schools and hospitals go to the Philippines to recruit Filipino workers and professionals as a way to lower their labor costs.

The Philippine government has failed to generate jobs so nursing graduates seek employment outside the country. Cartoon source: Bulatlat.com.

What are the rural and urban contexts of the forced migration of Filipinos?

In rural areas in the Philippines, powerful landlords, multinational agribusiness and mining corporations own or control most of the land, displacing millions of peasants. Some of the peasants become seasonal migrant farm workers and fisherfolks and the majority are landless rural poor. Others move to the cities to look for odd jobs.

In Philippine urban centers, workers—many from peasant background—seek employment in factories, construction, and service industries. But the majority of them cannot find work in the very few manufacturing and packaging factories in the cities. Many look for work abroad. For instance, some become seafarers and domestic workers.

Figure 1. The Structure of Filipino Migration to the United States

The Philippine government has failed to provide basic industrial infrastructure, making conditions very difficult for even trained or skilled workers to find work. Similarly thousands of graduates from colleges and universities in the medical, engineering, teaching and other professions are not able to find work or work with adequate wages commensurate to their training. As a result, workers and professionals are forced to seek employment abroad to seek a better life.

What role does the Philippine government have in exporting Filipino labor?

For over a century, Filipinos arrived on the north American continent through labor export systems that were promoted and regulated by a series of Spanish colonial administrators, U.S. military governor-generals, U.S. commonwealth administrators, and Philippine presidents.

Under Spanish colonial rule, Filipino slave laborers and indentured seafarers worked on the galleon trade between Manila and Acapulco in Mexico. Some escaped their forced labor, hid among the Louisiana bayous, and formed one of the earliest known Filipino communities on the north American continent. From the early 1900s to the 1930s, U.S. colonial and commonwealth administrators in the Philippines allowed companies operating plantations and canneries in Hawai'i, Alaska, California, and others areas on the U.S. continent to recruit laborers from the Philippines. Many came from the northern Luzon provinces of Ilocos Norte, Ilocos Sur, La Union, and Abra. In addition in the 1930s and 1940s, the U.S. Navy recruited Filipinos to work as mess cooks and compartment clearers.

More importantly, the Philippine government promotes and regulates the forced systematic migration of Filipinos worldwide that has resulted in significant modern day global migration of Filipinos. Since 1974, it has operated the **labor export program (LEP)** and policy, which exports Filipino workers as commodities in a systematic manner. In other words, this government program actively packages and sells Filipino migrant workers to businesses outside the Philippines. The government hopes to receive increased remittances from these exported laboring Filipinos to improve the national economy.

Formally, the program allows successive government agencies to act as brokers by marketing, selling, and exporting Filipino migrant workers and to manage their training, deployment, welfare, and return. A good number of migrants currently residing in the United States went through this program.

Furthermore, the labor export policy of successive Philippine presidents has shaped and affected the migration for many other Filipinos now residing in the U.S., even if these migrants did not go through the formal labor export program. Their migration experiences have still been structured due to the Philippine government's coercive labor export mechanism that binds together the interests of the U.S. government and U.S. businesses and allows for increased recruitment of Filipino workers and professionals. As a result, the largest group

> **The largest group of Filipinos working and living outside the Philippines is in the United States.**
>
> **Filipinos are the second largest immigrant group in the United States.**

of Filipinos working and living outside the Philippines is in the United States. Filipino migrants also have become the second largest immigrant group in the United States.

How does the U.S. government regulated Filipino migration into the U.S.?

In 1965, the U.S. government revamped its immigration law to standardize the country's recruitment of labor from other countries including the Philippines by instituting a formal mechanism that ranked occupations based on corporate demand. (Table 1 provides a brief timeline highlighting major events and laws affecting Filipino migration into the

Table 1. Major Events in U.S. Filipino Migration

1760s	Filipino slaves escaped their Spanish colonial masters and settled in present-day Louisiana.
1898	U.S. began military and administrative occupation of the Philippines
1903	The Pensionado Act allowed Filipino college students to enter the U.S.
1907+	A systematic recruitment of Filipino agricultural workers and manual laborers to the U.S. (and Hawaii) was instituted. Their presence prompted anti-Filipino riots later. Filipino workers in the U.S. formed mutual support organizations and joined labor unions.
1931	Filipinos in the U.S. armed forces became eligible for U.S. citizenship.
1934	The Morrison v. California decision made Filipinos ineligible for U.S. citizenship.
1934	The Tydings McDuffie Act promised independence to the Philippines after a ten-year commonwealth period and assigned an annual quota of 50 Filipinos to enter the U.S.
1935	The U.S. Congress passed Repatriation Bill to encourage Filipinos to return to the Philippines.
1945-50	The War Brides Act allowed Filipinas who married U.S. Armed Forces personnel and settle in the U.S.
1946	The U.S. granted Philippines "independence."
1946	The Philippine Trade Act granted nonquota immigrant status to Philippine citizens, their spouses, and children who have resided in the U.S. for a continuous period of three years prior to November 30, 1941.
1946	The Filipino Naturalization Act (also known as the Luce-Cellar Act) conferred the right of naturalization and set annual immigration quota of 100 for Filipinos.
1946	The Rescission Act deemed that U.S. Filipino World War Two veterans did not engaged in military service, and therefore did not deserve full veteran equity benefits.
1965	The Immigration and Naturalization Act increased the quota for Filipinos through family unification and professional worker provisions.
1972	Marcos declared martial law in the Philippines, forcing many to seek political refugee status in the U.S.
1974	The Marcos regime in the Philippines enacted the Labor Export Program (LEP) to consolidate its systematic export of Filipino workers and professionals as commodities to work in other countries and use their remittances to finance the underdeveloped Philippine economy.
1976	The Health Professionals Education Assistance Act reduced influx of foreign doctors, nurses, and pharmacists. The Eilberg Act of 1977 further restricted immigration of professionals.
1986	The Marcos regime collapsed.
1986	The Immigra.on Reform and Control Act penalized employers for hiring undocumented workers while provided amnesty to the undocumented who can prove they worked and resided in the U.S. before 1982.
1996	The Illegal Immigrant Reform and Individual Responsibility Act (IIRIRA) moved to criminalize and deport U.S. Filipinos who are contract workers, immigrants, and U.S. citizens.
2002	The Uniting and Strengthening America by Providing Appropriate Tools Required to Intercept and Obstruct Terrorism (U.S.A. PATRIOT) Act and the Homeland Security Act allowed for the implementation of IIRIRA in an expanded manner.

U.S.) In the 1970s and 1980s, Filipino nurses and other healthcare workers and professionals entered the U.S. through this occupational preference mechanism. This law also allowed for a formal mechanism to unify migrant families. Some supporters of the family unification provision believed that it would curtail what they saw as the surges in questionable new marriages between U.S. Whites and non-White immigrants such as Filipinos that would result in new family arrangements.

The 1996 Illegal Immigration Reform and Immigrant Responsibility Act (IIRIRA), implemented by President Clinton, dramatically shifted immigrant rights (see CFFSC 2004). IIRIRA curtailed unauthorized immigration and regulated immigrants, regardless of status, making a home in the U.S. The passing of the Uniting and Strengthening America by Providing Appropriate Tools Required to Intercept and Obstruct Terrorism (USA PATRIOT) Act and the establishment of Homeland Security after September 11, 2001 subsume the regulation of immigration into national security.

Shifts in U.S. legislation have produced difficulty in the lives of U.S. Filipinos, regardless of citizenship status. U.S. Filipinos have been unduly targeted for unjust removal, destructively detained, and placed under detrimental legal uncertainties. They are struggling against new forms of family hardship, and living through legislatively-generated fear and harassment.

2 National Profile of U.S. Filipinos and Their Common Concerns

What is the general profile of Filipinos in U.S. society?

In 2008, there is an estimated four million Filipinos residing in the United States, which accounts for 1.4 percent of the total U.S. population. They remain a predominantly immigrant group. Two of three Filipinos in the U.S. were born in the Philippines. Twenty percent of current residing Filipinos first entered the U.S.

4
MILLION U.S. FILIPINOS

FILIPINOS AS PERCENT OF U.S. POPULATION
1.4%

PERCENT FILIPINAS
54%
REFLECTING RECRUITMENT OF WOMEN FROM THE PHILIPPINES

PERCENT BORN IN IN THE PHILIPPINES
65%

PERCENT UNDOCUMENTED
24%

MEDIAN AGE
34
YEARS OLD, YOUNGER THAN U.S. AVERAGE

PERCENT U.S. CITIZEN
26%

TYPICAL FAMILY SIZE
3.7
MORE THAN U.S. AVERAGE

PERCENT CONVERSANT IN A PHILIPPINE LANGUAGE
57%

Figure 2. National Profile of U.S. Filipinos in Words and Numbers

Table 2. National Overview of U.S. Filipinos

	U.S. Filipinos	Total U.S. Population
Population, estimated 2008	4,135,000	305,746,000
U.S. census estimate	3,151,000	
Uncounted & undocumented	984,000	
Family	622,880	75,119,260
Average family size	3.7	3.2
Age		
Under 17 years	27%	24%
Under 34 years	51%	48%
65 and over	9%	12%
Median age (years)	34	37
School enrollment, 3 years & over enrolled in school		
Pre-school, nursery, kindergarten	10%	11%
Elementary school	39%	41%
High school	20%	22%
College or graduate school	31%	26%
Educational attainment, for 25 years and over		
Less than high school diploma	8%	16%
Bachelor's degree	38%	17%
Graduate or professional degree	9%	10%
Citizenship status, for non-U.S. born		
Non-U.S. citizen	60%	42%
Naturalized U.S. citizen	40%	58%

Source: U.S. Census 2007 American Community Survey, National Bulosan Center Research

after 1999. Approximately one million U.S. Filipinos—which is about 24 percent—lack legal resident documents or were not officially counted by the U.S. Census.

There are more U.S. Filipinas than Filipino men, a gendered pattern reflecting the greater demand for the labor of young women from the Philippines. About 53.6 percent are Filipinas and 46.4 percent are Filipino men. Furthermore as a group, U.S. Filipinos tend to be a bit younger

compared to the general population in the U.S. The median age for Filipinos is 33.6 years, about 2.3 years less than residents in the U.S. Twenty-seven percent of U.S. Filipinos are under 18 years and nine percent are 65 years and older.

Filipino families are typically bigger in terms of family size relative to the U.S. norm. There are about six hundred thousand Filipino families in the U.S. with an average family size of 3.7 members,

Table 3. Top Ranked U.S. Census Regions with Large Number of Filipinos

	General Population	Number of Filipinos[1]	Number of Filipino Families
Census-Defined Regions			
Los Angeles, Riverside, Orange county CA region	16,373,645	434,781	91,796
San Francisco, San Jose, Oakland, CA region	7,039,362	379,196	76,396
Honolulu, HI region	876,156	191,393	41,544
NYC, North NJ, Long Island, NY region	21,199,865	176,902	38,198
San Diego, CA region	2,813,833	145,132	29,162
Chicago, IL-Gary, IN-Kenosha, WI region	9,157,540	95,298	20,738
Seattle, Tacoma, Bremerton, WA region	3,554,760	80,112	15,887
Washington, DC-Baltimore, MD-VA-WV region	7,608,070	58,771	11,975
Las Vegas, NV-AZ region	1,563,282	42,596	8,787
Sacramento-Yolo, CA region	1,796,857	39,826	8,049
U.S.A.	281,421,906	2,364,815	472,050

Note: (1) This is official U.S. census tally, which does not include undocumented residence and people who are not officially counted. Source: U.S. Census 2000 SF-2 (Tables DP-1 and QT-P10)

which are somewhat larger than the typical 3.2-member family. The 622,880 Filipino families include heterosexually married-couple families (75 percent), female householder with no husband present (17 present), and people living alone (22 percent). Filipino households have higher percentages with siblings (2.3 percent compared to 1.1 percent overall), with parents (2.4 percent compared to 0.9 percent), with other relatives (12.5 percent compared to 5.6 percent), and with non-relatives (6.2 percent compared to 5.3 percent) living in the same household.

Many families transmit cultural heritage through Filipino language. Still, some struggle to gain proficiency in English and others opt to speak primarily in English. Among Filipinos at least five years old living in United States, 60 percent spoke a language from the Philippines at home and with family, relatives, and friends. About 40 percent of U.S. Filipinos chose to converse only English. Twenty percent reported that they do not speak English "very well."

Table 2 provides the general demographics on U.S. Filipinos. Tables 3, 4, and 5 highlight their geographic concentration and social, housing, educational, and economic conditions regionally.

Table 4. U.S. Urban Areas with the Largest Concentration of Filipinos With Over 16,000 in Population

Census-Defined U.S. Urban Areas	Number of U.S. Filipinos[1]	Percent Filipinos in the Urban Area
Honolulu, HI	170,219	23.7
Vallejo, CA	30,157	19.0
Stockton, CA	22,189	7.1
San Francisco-Oakland, CA	205,224	6.9
San Jose, CA	85,461	5.6
San Diego, CA	143,489	5.4
Las Vegas, NV	41,272	3.1
Los Angeles-Long Beach-Sta Ana, CA	348,263	3.0
Sacramento, CA	34,480	2.5
Seattle, WA	62,729	2.3
Virginia Beach, VA	29,002	2.1
Riverside-San Bernardino, CA	28,215	1.9
Chicago, IL	91,595	1.1
Washington, DC-VA-MD	43,236	1.1
New York, Newark, NY-NJ-CT	166,597	0.9
Houston, TX	24,511	0.6
Phoenix-Mesa, AZ	16,103	0.6
Philadelphia, PA, NJ-DE-MD	19,708	0.4

Note: (1) This is official U.S. census tally, which does not include undocumented residence and people who are not officially counted. Source: U.S. Census 2000

What are the common concerns of Filipinos in U.S. society?

In general, Filipinos in the United States face the following unique social ills, resulting in their economic, cultural, and political under-development:

1. Filipinos facing **U.S. economic injustice:** The U.S. economic system with the compliant Philippine state promotes Filipinos to seek employment in the U.S. Many who arrive—while college educated and professionally skilled—work in low-income and semi-skilled jobs. The ruling economic system causes the suffering of U.S. Filipinos. This system has no genuine interest in developing Filipinos and their communities to be truly self-reliant and independent. To further its economic and political dominance, the U.S. economic

Table 5. Social, Household, Education, and Economic Overview, By U.S. Census Regions

	USA		Los Angeles, Riverside, Orange Cnty CA		SF, SJ, Oakland, CA		Honolulu, HI region		NYC, N. NJ, Long Island NY, CT, PA	
	Filipinos	All	Filipinos	All	Filipinos	All	Filipinos	All	Filipinos	All
Social Demographics										
Percent total Filipinos		0.7		2.7		5.4		21.8		0.8
Percent women	54.1*	50.9	53.8*	50.4	52.9*	50.2	50.8*	49.7	55.9*	51.9
Average age (years)	31.3	35.3	33.1*	32.4	32.9	35.6	29.7	35.7	34.6	35.9
Percent over 65 years old	7.6	12.4	8.9	9.9	9.2	11.1	9.4	13.4	6.5	12.7
Percent over 65 for women	3.2	7.3	5.3	5.8	5.5	6.5	4.9	7.5	4.2	7.6
Percent over 65 for men	4.4	5.1	3.6	4.2	3.7	4.6	4.5	5.9	2.4	5.0
Percent disabled, age 5-20 yrs	6.2	8.1	5.8	7.5	6.1	17.2	6.1	6.5	6.7	9.2
Percent disabled, age 21-64 yrs	19.6*	19.2	20.1	20.8	21.6	28.8	20.8*	16.8	18.9	20.2
Percent disabled, over 65 yrs	47.1*	41.9	50.7*	43.1	47.6*	40.2	46.4*	40.4	44.7*	40.0
Family and Household										
Percent now married, except separated	56.2*	54.4	55.3*	51.6	55.1*	51.8	53.6*	53.4	57.0*	51.2
Average family size	3.7*	3.1	3.8*	3.6	4.0*	3.3	4.2*	3.5	3.7*	3.3
Percent household with brother & sister of head of household	2.3*	1.1	2.7*	2.1	3.1*	1.8	2.3*	1.5	2.7*	1.7
Percent household with parent of head of household	2.4*	0.9	3.1*	1.6	3.0*	1.4	2.2*	1.7	2.8*	1.4
Percent household with other relatives of head of household, not including spouse & children	12.5*	5.6	13.7*	9.7	16.0*	7.9	7.8*	4.2	12.0*	7.6
Percent household with non-relatives of head of household	6.2*	5.3	5.8	6.5	6.9*	2.3	7.2*	6.2	5.7*	5.2
Percent of grandparent responsible for grandchildren	21.8	42.0	20.7	30.0	19.5	29.3	22.9	28.1	18.1	31.8
Housing										
Percent rented housing	41.5*	33.8	44.2	45.2	39.0	42.2	43.9	45.4	47.0	47.0
Average household size of owner-occupied housing	3.7*	2.7	3.9*	3.1	4.1*	2.8	4.5*	3.1	3.7*	2.9
Average household size of rented housing	2.9*	2.4	2.9	2.9	3.1	2.5	3.5	2.7	2.6	2.5
Median value of owner-occupied unit (in thousands)	185.7	119.6	198.1	203.3	303.0	353.5	262.7	309.0	199.5	203.1
Median monthly mortgage	1,530*	1,088	1,641*	1,494	1,834*	1,822	2,620*	1,806	1,875*	1,679
Median monthly rent	727*	608	742*	733	947	968	750	802	875*	740
Median year built, owner-occupied unit	1977	1971	1973	1968	1974	1967	1977	1972	1959	1958
Median year built, rented housing	1972	1969	1972	1968	1969	1965	1972	1971	1956	1954
Median year moved in, owner-occupied	1993	1991	1993	1991	1992	1990	1990	1972	1992	1988
Median year moved in, rented housing	1998	1998	1998	1997	1997	1997	1997	1971	1996	1996
Median rooms, owner occupied unit	5.7	6.1	5.4	5.8	5.6	6.0	5.1	5.2	6.1	6.4
Median rooms, rented	3.1	4.0	2.6	3.3	3.1	3.4	3.1	3.3	3.1	3.5
Average occupants per room, owner-occupied unit	0.66*	0.43	0.72*	0.53	0.73*	0.47	0.87*	0.60	0.62*	0.44
Average occupants per room, rented housing	0.85*	0.59	0.98*	0.86	0.80*	0.66	0.99*	0.76	0.80*	0.66

Note: A "*" symbol indicates overrepresentation compared to the general population.
Source: U.S. Census 2000 SF-2 (Table QT-1) and SF-4 (Tables QT-2, QT-3, QT-4).

(Con't Next Page)

	San Diego, CA region		Chicago, IL-Gary, IN-Kenosha, WI		Seattle, Tacoma, Bremerton, WA		Washington, DC-Baltimore, MD, VA, WV rgn		Las Vegas, NV, AZ region		Sacramento-Yolo, CA region	
	Filipinos	All	Filipinos	All	Filipinos	All	Filipinos	All	Filipinos	All	Filipinos	All
Social Demographics												
Percent total Filipinos		5.2		1.0		2.3		0.8		2.7		2.2
Percent women	52.9*	49.7	54.6*	51.1	53.4*	50.2	56.7*	51.5	53.9*	49.2	53.3*	51.0
Average age (years)	31.2	33.2	32.6	33.9	29.6	35.3	32.8	35.4	31.6	35.2	28.9	34.6
Percent over 65 years old	8.6	11.2	7.1	10.9	6.3	10.3	6.1	10.1	6.6	11.8	7.3	11.3
Percent over 65 for women	5.0	6.4	4.4	6.5	3.7	6.0	2.4	6.0	3.8	6.2	4.1	6.5
Percent over 65 for men	3.6	4.7	2.1	4.4	2.6	4.3	3.7	4.1	2.8	5.6	3.2	4.8
Percent disabled, age 5-20 yrs	5.3	7.1	6.4	7.7	6.5	7.5	6.8	7.9	7.1	8.0	5.5	7.7
Percent disabled, age 21-64 yrs	19.8*	17.9	18.1*	17.3	18.9*	16.8	15.3	16.2	23.6*	23.0	17.7	19.5
Percent disabled, over 65 yrs	47.5*	40.8	43.4*	40.7	51.2*	41.3	44.2*	39.1	39.2	40.9	50.6*	41.5
Family and Household												
Percent now married, except separated	56.8*	52.0	56.7*	52.2	55.7*	54.2	56.7*	52.2	57.7*	53.3	53.1*	52.6
Average family size	3.9*	3.3	3.7*	3.3	3.6*	3.1	3.5*	3.2	3.6*	3.1	3.6*	3.2
Percent household with brother & sister of head of household	2.2*	1.4	2.7*	1.6	1.9*	0.9	2.0*	1.3	2.5*	1.6	2.0*	1.2
Percent household with parent of head of household	2.7*	1.1	2.7*	1.0	1.9*	0.7	2.0*	1.0	2.5*	1.3	2.1*	1.0
Percent household with other relatives of head of household, not including spouse & children	5.4*	2.6	5.1*	2.4	9.9*	4.0	4.5*	2.0	5.0*	2.5	4.0*	1.8
Percent household with non-relatives of head of household	5.5	7.5	5.0*	4.7	5.8	6.8	8.0*	6.2	7.6	7.7	7.0*	6.6
Percent of grandparent responsible for grandchildren	22.1	32.4	14.2	37.7	24.8	39.2	23.5	39.4	26.4	41.2	26.9	38.5
Housing												
Percent rented housing	42.2	44.6	34.1	34.8	40.2*	37.1	36.1*	35.0	40.6*	38.9	40.8*	38.7
Average household size of owner-occupied housing	4.0*	2.8	3.5*	2.9	3.6*	2.7	3.4*	2.7	3.7*	2.7	3.5*	2.7
Average household size of rented housing	3.1*	2.7	2.5*	2.4	2.7	2.2	2.5*	2.3	2.9*	2.5	2.8*	2.5
Median value of owner-occupied unit (in thousands)	192.9	227.2	183.0*	159.0	174.1	195.4	170.3*	161.6	140.7*	136.2	146.8	159.7
Median monthly mortgage	1,579*	1,541	1,595*	1,347	1,420*	1,399	1,530*	1,382	1,200*	1,157	1,328*	1,298
Median monthly rent	726	761	695*	659	696	723	816*	744	688	703	680*	673
Median year built, owner-occupied unit	1982	1975	1972	1964	1979	1974	1980	1973	1995	1990	1985	1977
Median year built, rented housing	1977	1974	1962	1959	1975	1974	1973	1969	1986	1986	1977	1974
Median year moved in, owner-occupied	1992	1992	1994	1991	1993	1992	1993	1991	1997	1996	1994	1992
Median year moved in, rented housing	1998	1998	1998	1997	1999	1998	1999	1998	1999	1999	1999	1998
Median rooms, owner occupied unit	5.8	5.9	6.0	6.2	5.9	6.4	6.7	7.1	5.5	5.7	6.0	6.0
Median rooms, rented	3.0	3.6	3.3	4.0	3.1	3.8	3.3	4.0	3.2	3.8	3.3	3.9
Average occupants per room, owner-occupied unit	0.69*	0.47	0.59*	0.46	0.59*	0.41	0.51*	0.38	0.63*	0.47	0.58*	0.44
Average occupants per room, rented housing	0.95*	0.73	0.72*	0.58	0.78*	0.56	0.71*	0.55	0.87*	0.65	0.77*	0.65

Note: A "*" symbol indicates overrepresentation compared to the general population.
Source: U.S. Census 2000 SF-2 (Table QT-1) and SF-4 (Tables QT-2, QT-3, QT-4).

(Con't Next Page)

	USA		Los Angeles, Riverside, Orange Cnty CA		SF, SJ, Oakland, CA		Honolulu, HI region		NYC, N. NJ, Long Island NY, CT, PA	
	Filipinos	**All**	**Filipinos**	**All**	**Filipinos**	**All**	**Filipinos**	**All**	**Filipinos**	**All**
Language and Education										
Percent language other than English (proxy for speaking a Philippine language for Filipinos)	58.8*	17.9	67. 0*	46.8	64.8*	35.9	45.6*	28.9	72.0*	33.5
Percent speak English less than "very well"	19.9*	8.1	20.9*	24.5	23.4*	17.3	23.0*	13.8	18.5*	15.6
Percent in linguistically isolated household in which all members 14 years old and over have at least some difficulty with English	7.7*	4.7	8.1	14.0	8.4	9.7	7.8*	6.4	7.5	9.2
Percent with no HS diploma over 25 years old	12.6	19.6	10.1	27.1	11.8	16.1	23.9*	15.0	5.9	20.6
Percent with BA/BS degree, over 25 years old	33.9*	15.5	40.7*	15.9	33.9*	23.2	14.1	18.9	51.9*	17.9
Percent with graduate or professional degree, over 25 years old	7.8	8.9	7.3	8.5	6.0	14.1	2.8	9.0	13.7*	12.6
Economic Conditions										
Percent in civilian labor force, over 16 years old	66.9*	63.9	65.7*	61.2	67.2*	65.9	64.7*	59.1	69.7*	61.8
Percent in civilian labor force for women over 16 years old	65.3*	57.4	63.8*	54.0	64.2*	59.5	63.5*	57.4	67.6*	55.2
Per capita income (dollars)	19259	21587	19458	21170	21239	30769	14545	21998	26587	26604
Median earnings for full-time, year-round employed men (dollars)	35419	37057	36670	38623	38967	50517	29886	36196	40335	45115
Median earnings for full-time, year-round employed women (dollars)	31061	27194	34194	31089	34568	37960	24233	29434	45275	34464
Percent family living below poverty	5.4	9.2	5.6	12.2	3.2	5.7	7.9*	7.0	3.2	10.2
Percent household with public assistance income	3.9	3.4	3.2	5.4	3.3*	3.1	11.3*	6.8	2.2	4.5
Percent household with retired income	12.6	16.7	10.1	13.7	13.6	15.6	19.8	21.9	7.1	15.6

Note: A "*" symbol indicates overrepresentation compared to the general population.
Source: U.S. Census 2000 SF-2 (Table QT-1) and SF-4 (Tables QT-2, QT-3, QT-4).

(Con't Next Page)

system underdevelops low-income and semi-skilled Filipinos through exploitation, political exclusion, cultural racism, and violent oppression.

Consequently this system fosters the **lack of meaningful work** with **decent pay** at a living wage, comprehensive personal and family **benefits**, and **dignity, respect, and fair treatment at work**: the *per capita income* for U.S. Filipinos was $25,644 in 2007 compared to $31,138 for non-Latino Whites. Also, compared to other workers, U.S. Filipinos tend to face specific forms of workplace discrimination due to often employers' incorrect perception of Filipinos' inadequate skills in English communication, Filipinos' inadequate formal education (even though they tend to be more educated than the general population), and Filipino values and practices.

	San Diego, CA region		Chicago, IL-Gary, IN-Kenosha, WI		Seattle, Tacoma, Bremerton, WA		Washington, DC-Baltimore, MD, VA, WV rgn		Las Vegas, NV, AZ region		Sacramento-Yolo, CA region	
	Filipinos	All	Filipinos	All	Filipinos	All	Filipinos	All	Filipinos	All	Filipinos	All
Language and Education												
Percent language other than English (proxy for speaking a Philippine language for Filipinos)	61.6*	33.0	67.8*	24.9	54.2*	14.6	61.9*	16.3	63.6*	24.1	48.4*	21.9
Percent speak English less than "very well"	22.9*	15.0	17.8*	12.0	19.2*	6.4	17.6*	6.8	20.7*	11.7	17.3*	10.3
Percent in linguistically isolated household in which all members 14 years old & over have at least some difficulty with English	8.2*	8.1	6.9	7.0	7.9*	3.8	6.5*	3.8	8.7*	7.2	7.4*	6.1
Percent with no HS diploma over 25 years old	14.3	16.4	6.3	18.9	12.8*	10.5	8.6	15.1	14.4	20.7	12.7	15.5
Percent with BA/BS degree, over 25 years old	29.0*	18.7	50.4*	18.2	28.6*	21.5	39.7*	20.8	24.6*	10.8	30.5*	17.6
Percent with graduate or professional degree, over 25 years old	4.0	10.9	11.7*	10.7	5.0	10.5	13.7	16.3	4.0	5.6	5.7	9.0
Economic Conditions												
Percent in civilian labor force, over 16 years old	61.6*	60.9	71.2*	65.7	70.5*	67.3	69.8*	65.3	66.5*	63.0	67.2*	63.8
Percent in civilian labor force for women over 16 years old	62.2*	56.2	69.5*	55.4	66.6*	61.6	71.5*	63.6	64.3*	57.4	65.6*	58.3
Per capita income (dollars)	16391	22926	24124	24581	17071	25744	22941	28175	16615	21210	17749	22302
Median earnings for full-time, year-round employed men (dollars)	31000	36952	37822	43821	33376	42259	40440	45204	28365	34627	35675	41070
Median earnings for full-time, year-round employed women (dollars)	27217	30356	38652*	31227	27832	31679	32046	34943	25066	26581	30612	31661
Percent family living below poverty	4.9	8.9	2.8	7.9	6.3	8.5	3.8	5.9	6.8	8.1	6.2	8.7
Percent household with public assistance income	4.0*	3.6	2.8	3.6	3.8*	3.2	1.3	2.4	2.7*	2.5	4.3	5.5
Percent household with retired income	22.6*	17.7	7.6	14.2	12.7	16.6	12.1	18.1	13.9	18.6	13.9	18.6

Note: A "*" symbol indicates overrepresentation compared to the general population.
Source: U.S. Census 2000 SF-2 (Table QT-1) and SF-4 (Tables QT-2, QT-3, QT-4).

Moreover, working Filipinos often send remittances to family members back to the Philippines, further reducing their ability to pay for their own food, shelter, and other basic needs. In 2005, over **60 percent of remittances** (around $5.32 billion) sent to the Philippines came from Filipinos working in the United States.

Low-income and semi-skilled U.S. Filipinos also often **lack long- and short-term affordable housing** and living arrangement: compared to others living in the country, these Filipinos face greater economic dependency on more well-off relatives in terms of housing. Due to low income and high housing cost, they face relative hardship and the difficulty of owning residential properties. Thirty-four percent of U.S. Filipinos rent, as compared to 26 percent for non-Latino Whites. The

DISPARITY IN
PER CAPITA INCOME

18% less

$25,644 FOR FILIPINOS
COMPARED TO $31,138 FOR
NON-LATINO WHITES IN 2007

DISPARITY IN
MONTHLY RENT

28% more

$999 MEDIAN RENT FOR
FILIPINOS COMPARED TO $782
NON-LATINO WHITES IN 2007

Figure 3. U.S. Filipinos Facing Economic Disparities in Words and Numbers

median monthly housing cost for U.S. Filipino renters is $999, as compared to $782 for non-Latino Whites. The average household size for rental units is 2.9 for U.S. Filipinos, as compared to 2.1 for non-Latino Whites. The average occupant per room in a rental unit is 0.66 for Filipinos compared to 0.43 for the general population. In addition, thirty-eight percent of U.S. Filipino renters spend 37 percent or more of household income on housing.

Moreover, low-income and semi-skilled U.S. Filipinos **lack adequate preventative and emergency health coverage**: compared to others in the nation, they tend to find the medical and health care system highly inaccessible and cost prohibitive due to their low income and other high living expenses (for transportation, utilities, food, child-rearing, and so on). The average life expectancy for U.S. Filipinos is 80.6 years. Over twenty percent of them lack any form of health insur-

ance. While many of them work in the frontline providing personal health services, they cannot obtain adequate care for themselves and their own immediate families in the U.S. and the Philippines.

2. **Anti-Filipino racism and bogus assimilation and Filipinos facing biased U.S. legal system**: Racism is the institutional practice and belief that the white racial group and culture is more worthy and superior to other groups and their ways of life, therefore these groups deserve less economic, political, and social benefits. White supremacy embedded in the U.S. social and economic fabric deploys various forms of racism on specific communities of color for its own economic and political benefits. It makes false promises of civil rights, democratic inclusion, and economic opportunities such as anti-discrimination laws. Instead it offers U.S. Filipinos and other racial-ethnic groups bogus assimilation into U.S. society,

Common Concerns of U.S. Filipinos

- Economic injustice
  - → Lack of meaningful work
  - → Lack of decent pay, work benefits, dignity, respect, and fair treatment at work
  - → Lack of long- and short-term affordable housing
  - → Lack of adequate preventative and emergency health coverage
- Racism, bogus assimilation & unjust U.S. legal system
- Family separation, unjust U.S. immigration policy & coercive Philippine labor export policy

unequal legal rights, and escalating the underdevelopment of Filipino communities.

This bogus assimilation and biased legal system are evident in post-9/11 immigration and national security policies. The legal system remains highly non-responsive to working Filipinos seeking support on immigration and related issues. Compared to others, working Filipinos continue to find it difficult to "sponsor" their children to come to the U.S. or to stay by getting proper residency documentation. They face the brunt of the racist enforcement of Department of Homeland Security policies that target and scrutinize Filipinos more, forcing many to hide publicly.

In additional, anti-Filipino racism promotes negative stereotypes and group invisibility across various social, political, economic, educational, and media institutions. This cultural racism encourages the belief that the prevailing ways of living in the United States are superior to those of Filipinos. Moreover, this cultural racism devalues Filipinos' attempts to engage in varying forms of cultural production.

3. **Government policies separate Filipino families across national borders**: The United States immigration policies promote separation of Filipino families, particularly due to the current visa system. Applicants from the Philippines have one of the longest waiting periods for visa processing—up to 25 years. Increasingly since September 11, 2001, deportation and inadmissibility orders from the Department of Homeland Security tear U.S. Filipino families apart as well. In addition, the Philippine government's labor export policy also separates families; it is complicit with U.S. government policies that separate Filipino families.

3 Economic Classes Among U.S. Filipinos

What are economic classes in the U.S.?

Economic classes are defined by groups' relations to ownership and control over what is produced and relations to possession and control over how things are produced. Groupings of U.S. Census-defined occupations serve as a handy general proxy for economic classes in the U.S. For U.S. Filipinos (see Table 6), the pertinent economic classes include:

1. **Workers**, which consist mostly low-income industrial, service, and agricultural workers and some moderate-income manufacturing, industrial and service worker:

   - *Manufacturing occupations* include assemblers and fabricators, food processing workers, metal workers and plastic workers, printing workers, textile, apparel, and furnishings workers, woodworkers, and plant and system operators.

   - *Industrial occupations* include hand laborers and material movers, motor vehicle operators, driver/sales workers and truck drivers, bus drivers, rail and water transportation workers, aircraft and traffic control occupation, carpenters, construction laborers, electricians, painters and paperhang-

   ers, pipelayers, plumbers, pipefitters, and steamfitters, construction traders workers except carpenters, electricians, painters, plumbers, and construction laborers, extraction workers, vehicle and mobile equipment mechanics, installers, and repairers, and electrical equipment mechanics.

   - *Service occupations* include cashiers, retail sales workers, personal appearance workers, transportation, tourism, and lodging attendants, child care workers, building and grounds cleaning and maintenance occupations, cooks and food preparation workers, waiters and waitresses, food and beverage serving workers, nursing, psychiatric, and home health aides, occupational and physical therapist assistants and aides, fire fighting and prevention workers, and protective service workers.

   - *Agricultural occupations* include agricultural workers and fishing, hunting, and forestry occupations.

2. **Professionals**, which consist mostly high-income and moderate-income service professionals, executives, and managers:

   - *Lower-level professional occupations* include counselors, social workers, and other community and social service specialists, religious

Table 6. Economic Profile of U.S. Filipinos

	U.S. Filipinos	Total U.S. Population
Economic class		
Workers[1]	45-54%	43%
Professionals[2]	40-46%	50%
Small and medium business owners	2-4%	7%
Big business owners[3]	0%	less than 1%
Transnational business and property owners[4]	less than 1%	
Top five low-income occupations, men		
1. Office & administrative support	14.6%	7.2%
2. Food preparation and server	5.3%	3.9%
3. Building & grounds cleaner	4.4%	3.7%
4. Personal care and service	1.9%	1.1%
5. Heathcare support	1.9%	0.4%
Top five low-income occupations, women		
1. Production occupation	7.5%	5.9%
2. Healthcare support	5.5%	3.8%
3. Building and grounds cleaner	3.4%	2.8%
4. Community & social service	1.0%	0.8%
5. Farming occupations	0.4%	0.3%
Top three low-income occupations, men		
1. Nursing & health diagnosing	4.9%	1.8%
2. Health technologist	2.1%	0.5%
3. Arts & entertainment	2.0%	1.9%
Top three low-income occupations, women		
1. Nursing & health diagnosing	14.6%	4.8%
2. Health technologist	3.8%	2.4%
3. Drafters	0.4%	0.2%

	U.S. Filipinos	Non-Latino Whites
Per Capita Income	$24,405	$29,406

Notes: (1) The category includes moderate-income and low-income industrial, service, and agricultural workers. See Table 8 for specific details. (2) This category includes high-income and moderate-income managers, executives, technical, and service professionals. See Table 10 for specific details. (3) This category includes U.S. owners and top executives who operate multinational businesses providing products and services to consumers in the U.S. and other countries. (4) This category includes the immediate family members of the top Philippine business and property conglomerates who reside in the U.S. and their owners, head executives, and lawyers when they stay and conduct business in the U.S. Source: U.S. Census 2006 American Community Survey, U.S. Census 2000

workers, preschool, kindergarten, elementary, middle school, secondary, postsecondary, and special education teachers, and librarians, curators, and archivists, services, wholesale and manufacturing sales representatives, communications equipment operators, financial clerks, except bookkeeping, accounting and auditing clerks, bookkeeping, accounting, and auditing clerks, customer service representative, material recording, scheduling, dispatching, and distributing worker, and secretaries and administrative assistants.

■ *Middle-level professional occupations* include construction and extraction workers supervisors, transportation, and material moving workers supervisors, life and physical scientists, social scientists, life, physical, and social science technicians, art and design workers, entertainers and performers, sports, and related workers, media and communications workers, registered nurses, therapists, other health diagnosing and treating practitioners and technical occupations, health technologists and technicians, and drafters, engineering, and mapping technicians.

■ *Top-level professional occupations* include top executives, financial managers, operations specialties managers, advertising, marketing, promotions, public relations, and sales managers, farmers and farm managers, business operations specialists, accountants and auditors, other financial specialists, computer specialists, mathematical science occupations, architects, surveyors, and cartographers, engineers, physicians and surgeons, judges, magistrates, and other judicial workers, and lawyers.

3. **Small and medium business owners,** which consist of self-employed people operating business and employed various number of workers:

■ Small business owners operate firms locally, often consisting of the self-employed owner and up to ten employees. These firms' annual revenue rarely exceeds one million dollars. These owners tend to operate, for instance, real estate and insurance franchise, restaurants, retail outlets, wholesale trade, and health services. Some are independent contractors.

■ Middle-level business owners operate firms with U.S. national and international reach, often with business capital assets up to $250 million.

Presently, no U.S. Filipino operates a big business and with a net worth of over $250 million. This fact highlights the limited opportunities for U.S. Filipino families to become part with the top tier of wealthy families in the U.S.

4. **Transnational business and property owners,** which consist of the immediate family members of the top Philippine business and property conglomerates who reside in the U.S. and their owners, head executives, and lawyers when they stay and conduct business in the U.S.

What is the social portrait of U.S. Filipino workers?

Two million (around 45 percent to 55 percent) U.S. Filipinos hold low income and semi-skilled jobs, limiting their social

Table 7. Top U.S. Industries Employing U.S. Filipinos, by Gender

Top Industry with Filipino Men	Top Industry with Filipinas
1. Manufacturing (15.3%)	1. Health care & social assistance (30.8%)*
2. Health care & social assistance (12.5%)*	2. Retail trade (11.0%)
3. Retail trade (11.0%)	3. Manufacturing (9.4%)
4. Accommodation & food services (8.4%)*	4. Accommodation & food services (7.7%)*
5. Transportation & warehousing (7.8%)*	5. Finance & insurance (7.4%)*

Note: A "*" symbol indicates overrepresentation compared to the general population. Source: U.S. Census 2000, SF-4 (Table P-30)

mobility and perpetuating their economic hardship. Many of them hold jobs such as: cashiers (3.24 percent of U.S. Filipinos), nursing, psychiatric, and home health aides (2.97 percent), retail salespersons (2.92 percent), maids and housekeeping cleaners (1.55 percent), customer service representatives (1.49 percent), janitors and building cleaners (1.44 percent), stock clerks and order fillers (1.42 percent), waiters and waitresses (1.26 per-cent), personal and home care aides (1.23 percent), cooks (1.17 percent), and hand laborers and freight, stock, and material movers (1.1 percent). Table 8 provides additional details on regional variations.

The U.S. government reports that 6.6 percent of U.S. Filipinos live in poverty. Around 7.1 percent of related children under 18 are below the poverty level, compared with 7.4 percent of people 65 years old and over. About 6.6 percent of all U.S. Filipino families and 13 percent of families with a female householder and no husband present had incomes below the poverty level. The actual percentage of U.S. Filipi-no living in poverty is higher than reported by the U.S. government.

RESILIENT COMMUNITIES U.S. Filipinos are *geographically clustered* into a limited number of neighborhoods, about one out of every 66 in the U.S. using census track boundaries. A majority of low-income and semi-skilled Filipinos resides in about 720 U.S. neighborhoods (see Table 9). Lower-middle income and professional Filipinos also reside closely in approximately 220 of these neighborhoods with their working-class compatriots.

Working-class communities typically consist of 40 percent of Filipinos living in rental units, 23.9 percent of Filipinos working in low-income service and clerical related occupations, 7.5 percent of Filipinos working in professional related occupations, and 2.9 percent of Filipinos working in production related occupations. In a typical area in 1999, Filipinos earned about on average $16,000.

Detailed analysis conducted by the National Bulosan Center shows that low-

Table 8. Occupational Concentration for Low-Income and Moderate-Income Worker Occupations, By Gender and Census Regions

MEN	USA		Los Angeles, Riverside, Orange Cnty CA		SF, SJ, Oakland, CA		Honolulu, HI region		NYC, N. NJ, Long Island, NY, CT, PA	
	% Filipinos	% All	% Filipinos	% All	% Filipinos	% All	% Filipinos	% All	% Filipinos	% All
TOTAL	**47.4**	**54.6**	**39.7**	**52.1**	**45.6***	**42.4**	**69.8***	**52.6**	**33.6**	**47.6**
Lower-Income Industrial, Service, and Agricultural Workers										
Healthcare support occupations	1.9*	0.4	2.5*	0.5	2.0*	0.4	0.7*	0.5	3.3*	0.6
Food preparation and serving related occupations	5.3*	3.9	3.3	4.1	3.6	3.6	11.2*	7.1	3.9	4.2
Building and grounds cleaning & maintenance occupations	4.4*	3.7	2.2	4.2	3.6	3.6	11.7*	5.2	2.7	3.9
Personal care and service occup.	1.9*	1.1	1.9*	1.3	1.7*	1.1	2.4*	2.2	1.2	1.3
Farming, fishing, & forestry occupations	0.7	1.1	0.1	0.7	0.2	0.7	1.4*	0.9	0.0	0.2
Moderate-Income Manufacturing, Industrial and Service Workers										
Protective service occupations	2.8	3.0	3.1*	2.8	2.8*	2.2	4.1	4.4	1.8	4.1
Lower-level sales occupations	4.4	5.4	4.9	5.7	4.8	5.3	3.8	5.1	4.5	5.9
Construction trades workers	3.4	8.6	2.2	7.4	2.3	6.9	9.3*	7.2	1.5	7.0
Extraction workers	0.0	0.2	0.0	0.0	0.0	0.0	0.0	0.0	0.0	0.0
Installation, maintenance & repair occup.	5.8	7.0	5.6	6.2	6.6*	5.1	7.8*	7.0	3.4	5.5
Production occupations	9.5	10.8	8.8	10.7	11.2*	6.9	6.3*	4.5	5.8	6.8
Aircraft & traffic control occup.	0.1	0.2	0.0	0.1	0.0	0.2	0.1	0.5	0.0	0.1
Motor vehicle operators	2.7	4.9	2.4	4.5	2.5	3.2	5.2*	4.2	2.6	5.0
Rail, water & other transportation occup.	0.6*	0.5	0.5*	0.4	0.9*	0.3	0.9*	0.8	0.5	0.6
Material moving workers	3.3	3.8	2.2	3.5	3.1*	2.5	4.9*	3.0	2.4	2.4

MEN	San Diego, CA region		Chicago, IL-Gary, IN-Kenosha, WI		Seattle, Tacoma, Bremerton, WA		Washington, DC-Baltimore, MD, VA, WV		Las Vegas, NV, AZ region		Sacramento-Yolo, CA region	
	% Filipinos	% All	% Filipinos	% All	% Filipinos	% All	% Filipinos	% All	% Filipinos	% All	% Filipinos	% All
TOTAL	**50.6***	**48.2**	**37.5**	**51.6**	**53.8***	**48.3**	**32.0**	**41.6**	**67.8***	**64.0**	**46.0**	**49.0**
Lower-Income Industrial, Service, and Agricultural Workers												
Healthcare support occupations	1.8*	0.5	3.0*	0.3	1.9*	0.5	0.8*	0.4	0.6*	0.3	2.7*	0.5
Food preparation and serving related occupations	5.4*	4.8	3.9*	3.8	5.7*	3.2	4.1*	3.6	19.3*	9.7	4.3*	4.2
Building and grounds cleaning & maintenance occupations	4.4	4.5	2.1	3.4	5.7*	3.2	3.5*	3.0	8.4*	5.3	4.6*	3.9
Personal care and service occup.	2.2*	1.4	1.6*	1.1	2.0*	1.1	1.5*	1.1	9.9*	6.3	1.7*	1.3
Farming, fishing, & forestry occup.	0.4	0.8	0.0	0.2	0.1	0.6	0.0	0.2	0.0	0.2	0.3	0.9
Moderate-Income Manufacturing, Industrial and Service Workers												
Protective service occupations	2.9	3.1	1.3	3.0	2.5*	2.3	1.6	3.6	3.9	4.4	3.5*	3.3
Lower-level sales occupations	3.9	5.7	4.0	5.7	3.8	5.5	4.6	4.7	5.5*	5.1	4.4	5.7
Construction trades workers	3.6	7.8	1.3	7.5	3.8	8.2	2.3	7.6	3.2	11.8	2.7	8.5
Extraction workers	0.0	0.0	0.0	0.0	0.1	0.0	0.0	0.0	0.0	0.2	0.0	0.1
Installation, maintenance & repair occup.	7.3*	6.2	4.1	6.0	6.4	6.6	6.0*	5.7	5.4	6.5	5.2	6.4
Production occupations	13.5*	7.0	10.4	10.9	12.4*	8.2	4.1	4.9	4.7	5.1	8.1*	6.0
Aircraft & traffic control occup.	0.2	0.3	0.1	0.2	0.0	0.4	0.1	0.2	0.1	0.4	0.0	0.2
Motor vehicle operators	1.8	3.5	2.1	4.8	2.5	3.9	1.3	3.9	3.3	5.3	2.8	4.1
Rail, water & other transportation occup.	0.2	0.4	0.7	0.6	0.6	0.6	0.3	0.4	0.5	0.6	0.5	0.4
Material moving workers	3.0*	2.2	2.9	4.1	4.2*	3.2	1.8	2.3	3.0*	2.8	5.2*	3.5

Note: A "*" symbol indicates overrepresentation compared to the general population.
Source: U.S. Census 2000 SF-4 (Tables QT-P28)

(Con't Next Page)

WOMEN	USA		Los Angeles, Riverside, Orange Cnty CA		SF, SJ, Oakland, CA		Honolulu, HI region		NYC, N. NJ, Long Island, NY, CT, PA	
	% Filipinas	% All Women	% Filipinas	% All Women	% Filipinas	% All Women	% Filipinas	% All Women	% Filipinas	% All Women
TOTAL	**33.4***	**32.9**	**23.8**	**32.8**	**30.4***	**27.1**	**45.2***	**32.0**	**18.5**	**28.2**
Lower-Income Industrial, Service, and Agricultural Workers										
Healthcare support occupations	5.5*	3.8	5.8*	3.0	6.4*	2.7	6.0*	3.0	4.6	5.0
Food preparation and serving related occupations	5.0	5.9	2.8	4.6	2.9	4.0	9.0*	7.0	1.6	3.5
Building and grounds cleaning & maintenance occupations	3.4*	2.8	1.3	3.1	2.1	2.5	9.6*	4.1	2.5	2.5
Personal care and service occup.	4.1	4.7	4.4	5.4	3.6	4.7	3.7	4.7	3.3	4.3
Farming, fishing, & forestry occup.	0.4*	0.3	0.0	0.3	0.0	0.0	1.1*	0.4	0.0	0.1
Moderate-Income Manufacturing, Industrial and Service Workers										
Protective service occupations	0.5	0.8	0.4	0.9	0.6	0.7	0.6	0.9	0.1	1.1
Lower-level sales occupations	5.4	6.0	4.5	6.2	5.1	5.5	8.4*	7.4	3.7	5.4
Construction trades workers	0.1	0.3	0.1	0.2	0.1	0.2	0.3*	0.2	0.1	0.2
Extraction workers	0.0	0.2	0.0	0.0	0.0	0.0	0.0	0.0	0.0	0.0
Installation, maintenance & repair occup.	0.3	0.4	0.2	0.4	0.5*	0.3	0.3	0.4	0.1	0.3
Production occupations	7.5*	5.9	3.5	6.7	7.9*	4.7	4.3*	2.5	2.3	4.3
Aircraft & traffic control occup.	0.0	0.0	0.0	0.0	0.0	0.0	0.0	0.0	0.0	0.0
Motor vehicle operators	0.2	0.8	0.1	0.6	0.1	0.5	0.6	0.6	0.1	0.6
Rail, water & other transportation occup.	0.1	0.1	0.1	0.1	0.1	0.1	0.1	0.1	0.0	0.1
Material moving workers	0.9	1.1	0.6	1.3	0.9*	0.8	1.2*	0.7	0.1	0.8

WOMEN	San Diego, CA region		Chicago, IL-Gary, IN-Kenosha, WI		Seattle, Tacoma, Bremerton, WA		Washington, DC-Baltimore, MD, VA, WV		Las Vegas, NV, AZ region		Sacramento-Yolo, CA region	
	% Filipinas	% All Women	% Filipinas	% All Women	% Filipinas	% All Women	% Filipinas	% All Women	% Filipinas	% All Women	% Filipinas	% All Women
TOTAL	**36.0***	**31.0**	**20.5**	**29.5**	**38.8***	**30.4**	**31.2***	**24.3**	**48.3***	**40.3**	**28.4***	**27.3**
Lower-Income Industrial, Service, and Agricultural Workers												
Healthcare support occupations	6.7*	3.1	5.0*	2.7	6.8*	3.2	3.7*	2.6	4.3*	2.2	5.6*	3.3
Food preparation and serving related occupations	4.8	5.2	2.0	4.5	7.3*	5.8	4.6*	4.1	10.5*	10.0	3.4	4.8
Building and grounds cleaning & maintenance occupations	2.4	3.2	1.2	2.3	3.8*	2.3	6.5*	2.7	8.5*	5.9	2.4*	2.2
Personal care and service occupa.	3.9	5.8	3.4	4.4	5.0	5.3	8.2*	4.6	10.8*	8.5	4.2	5.2
Farming, fishing, & forestry occup.	0.0	0.2	0.0	0.1	0.1	0.1	0.0	0.1	0.1*	0.0	0.2	0.4
Moderate-Income Manufacturing, Industrial and Service Workers												
Protective service occupations	0.7	0.8	0.2	1.0	0.3	0.7	0.3	1.2	0.5	1.1	0.5	0.9
Lower-level sales occupations	5.3	6.3	3.8	6.1	5.6	5.9	4.5	5.0	9.6*	7.8	4.1	5.3
Construction trades workers	0.1	0.3	0.1	0.2	0.0	0.5	0.1	0.2	0.1	0.5	0.0	0.3
Extraction workers	0.0	0.0	0.0	0.0	0.0	0.0	0.0	0.0	0.0	0.0	0.0	0.0
Installation, maintenance & repair occup.	0.3	0.5	0.3	0.4	0.6	0.6	0.3	0.4	0.3	0.3	0.4	0.5
Production occupations	11.0*	4.2	4.0	5.7	6.9*	3.7	2.6*	2.3	2.2	2.2	6.7*	2.8
Aircraft & traffic control occupa.	0.0	0.0	0.0	0.0	0	0.1	0.0	0.0	0.0	0.0	0.0	0.0
Motor vehicle operators	0.1	0.6	0.0	0.6	0.1	0.9	0.1	0.6	0.2	0.8	0.4	0.6
Rail, water & other transportation occup.	0.0	0.1	0.0	0.1	0.1	0.1	0.0	0.0	0.1	0.1	0.0	0.0
Material moving workers	0.7	0.7	0.5	1.4	2.1*	1.0	0.3	0.5	1.1*	0.9	0.5	1.0

Note: A "*" symbol indicates overrepresentation compared to the general population.
Source: U.S. Census 2000 SF-4 (Tables QT-P28)

Communities with
large concentration
of low income
U.S. Filipinos

Figure 4. Communities with Large Concentration of Low Income U.S. Filipinos.

**Table 9. Low and Lower-Middle Income
U.S. Filipino Communities, By U.S. States**

U.S. State	Low Income Areas	Areas With Mostly Low With Some Lower-Middle Income	Areas With Mostly Lower-Middle With Some Low Income
Hawaii	83	23	21
California	79	262	168
Nevada	8	1	1
Washington	6	18	2
Alaska	3	1	0
Illinois	2	4	6
Maryland	1	1	1
South Carolina	1	0	0
Virginia	0	11	3
Florida	0	4	2
New Jersey	0	2	10
Texas	0	1	2
New York	0	0	10
Total	**183**	**328**	**226**
% Service Workers	40.2	23.2	18.6
Average Earnings ($)	12,900	16,500	18,600

Source: U.S. Census 2000, National Bulosan Center Research

Members and friends of KABALIKAT, a domestic workers organizing project in Queens, New York.

income Filipinos reside in predominantly urban and in some rural areas—represented by the dots in Figure 4—in the West Coast of the U.S. such as Honolulu (HI), Vallejo (CA), San Francisco-Daly City-Oakland (CA), Seattle-Tacoma (WA), Stockton (CA), Delano (CA), Monterey (CA), Oxnard (CA), Los Angeles (CA), San Diego (CA), and Anchorage (AK), reflecting pre-1965 migration and pre-1965 community development as well as more recent migration into Concord (CA), Sacramento (CA), Lake Tahoe (CA), Reno (NV), Las Vegas (NV), Chicago (IL), Colmar Manor (MD), and Charleston (SC). In several regions, the three types of neighborhood—which are the (1) low income areas, (2) mostly low with some lower-middle income areas, and (3) mostly lower-middle with some low income areas—are highly contiguous. In contrast, there is less geographic clustering

in New York, New Jersey, Illinois, Virginia, and Maryland/Washington, DC. New communities are developing in Texas, Florida, and even South Carolina.

Figures 5, 6, 7, 8, 9, 10, 11, 12, 13, 14, 15, 16, 17, 18, 19, 20, and 21 depict census tract areas with relatively high concentration of low and lower-middle income Filipinos for metropolitan and rural areas across the United States.

While many low-income and semi-skilled Filipinos reside often in particular geographic locations, a good number are scattered within areas with smaller concentration of Filipinos. Often they live in *relative cultural isolation* away from sizeable Filipino communities because of labor recruitment and as military and correspondent, also known as "pen-pal" brides.

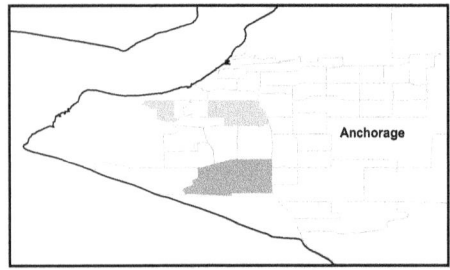

Figure 5. Filipino Communities in Anchorage, Alaska.

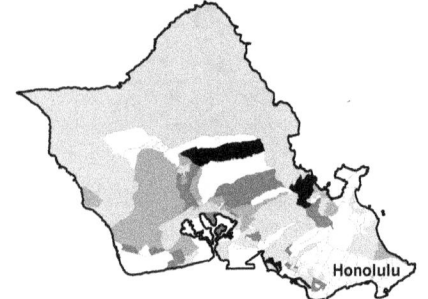

Figure 6. Filipino Communities in Honolulu, Hawai`i.

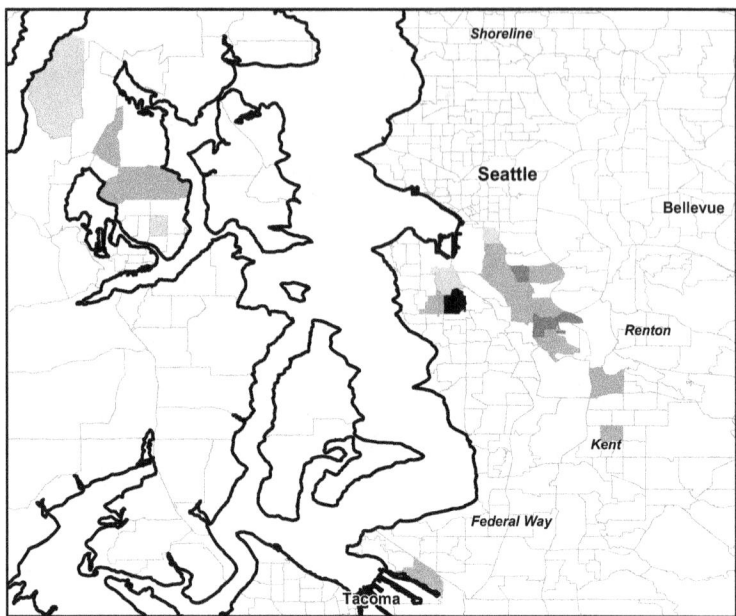

Figure 7. Filipino Communities in the Seattle-Tacoma region in Washington.

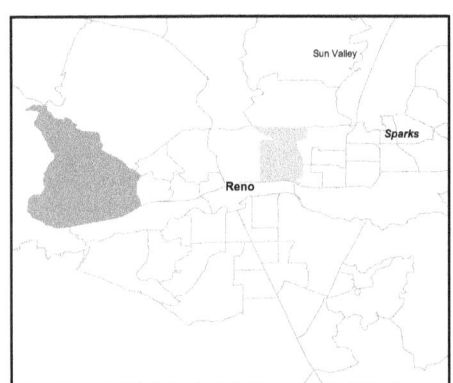

Figure 8. Filipino Communities in Reno, Nevada.

MAP LEGEND
for Figure 5 to Figures 21

Area With
Low Income Filipinos

Area With Mostly Low With Some
Lower-Middle Income Filipinos

Area With Mostly Lower-Middle
With Some Low Income Filipinos

Area With Lower-Middle
Income Filipinos

Area With Few
Or No Filipinos

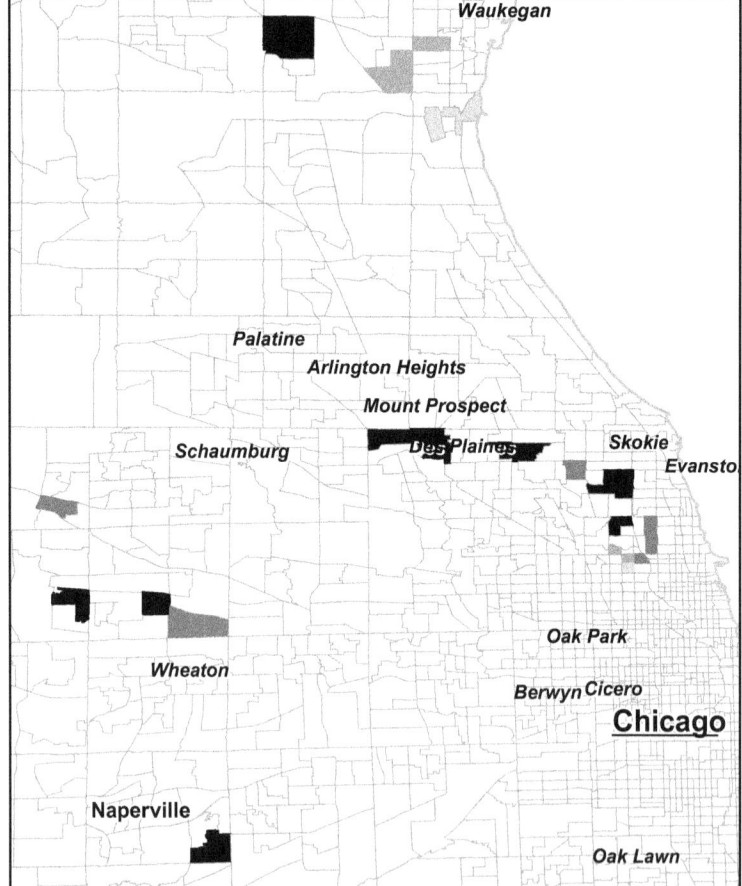

Figure 9. Filipino Communities in the Chicago region in Illinois.

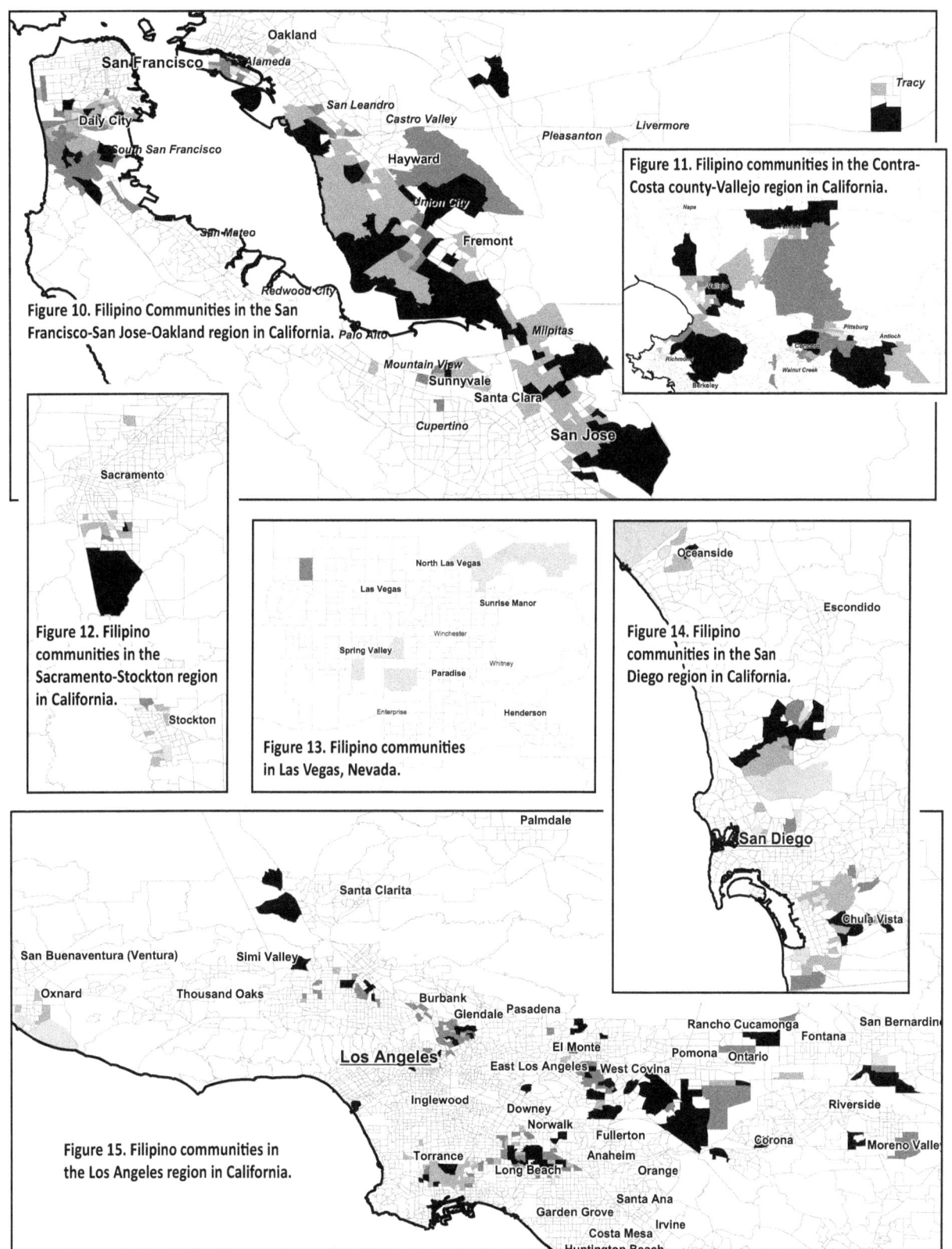

Figure 10. Filipino Communities in the San Francisco-San Jose-Oakland region in California.

Figure 11. Filipino communities in the Contra-Costa county-Vallejo region in California.

Figure 12. Filipino communities in the Sacramento-Stockton region in California.

Figure 13. Filipino communities in Las Vegas, Nevada.

Figure 14. Filipino communities in the San Diego region in California.

Figure 15. Filipino communities in the Los Angeles region in California.

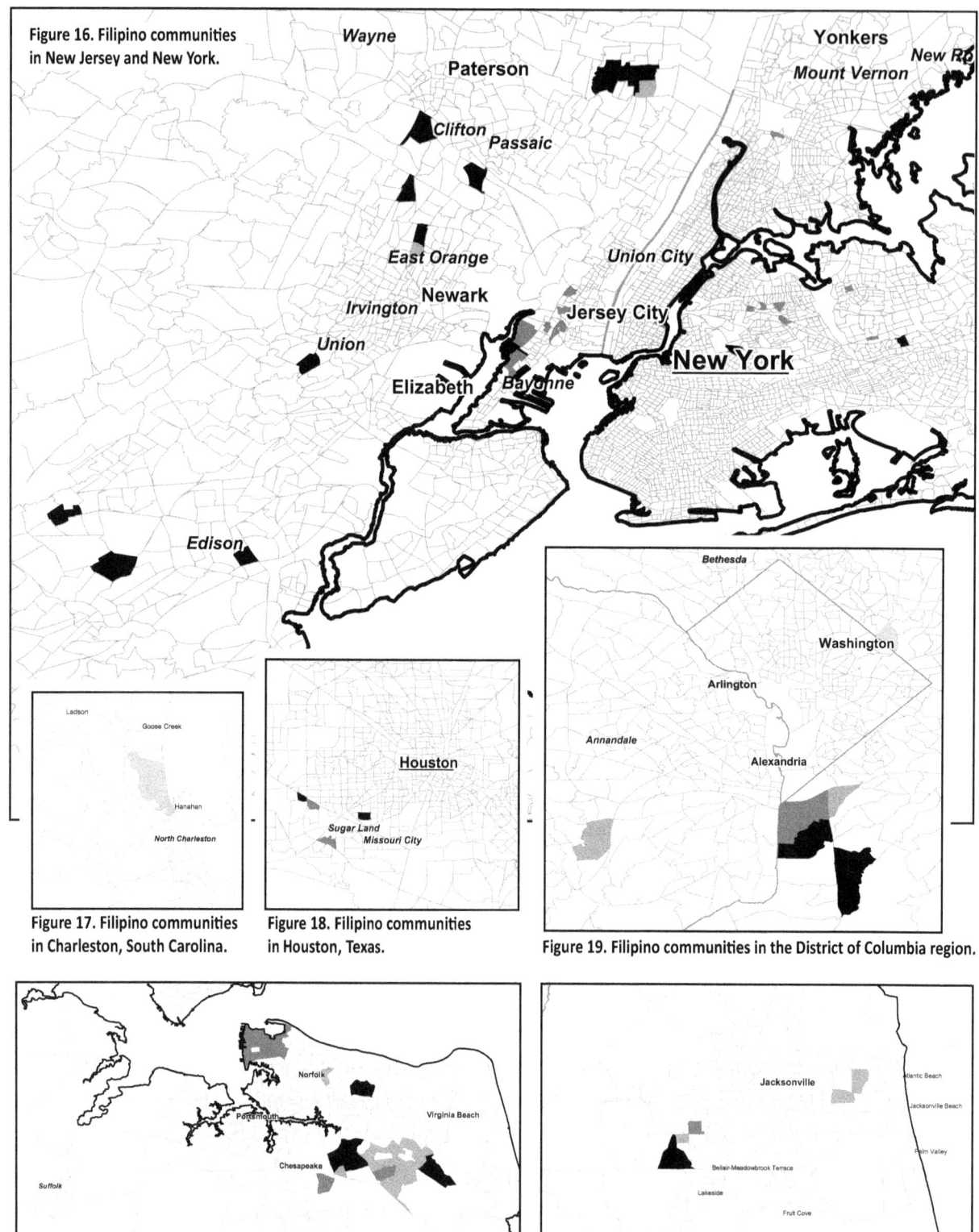

Figure 16. Filipino communities in New Jersey and New York.

Figure 17. Filipino communities in Charleston, South Carolina.

Figure 18. Filipino communities in Houston, Texas.

Figure 19. Filipino communities in the District of Columbia region.

Figure 20. Filipino communities in the Norfolk-Virginia Beach region in Virginia.

Figure 21. Filipino communities in Jacksonville, Florida.

What are specific issues among selected U.S. Filipino workers?

The following illustrates some the—often invisible— working and economic conditions of low-income and semi-skilled Filipinos, specifically those who are domestic and home care workers, airport workers, and seafarers.

DOMESTIC AND HOME CARE WORKERS

There are over 30,000 Filipinas and Filipino men employed as domestic and home care workers. They range from in-live nanny, personal attendants, caregivers, out-live domestic workers, child-care worker, senior-care worker, patient care worker, and home cleaners and housekeeper. They regularly perform a range of tasks including cleaning, cooking, washing dishes and laundry, personal care, and shopping. Many of them face hardships at work due to low wage and lack of benefits, expectations of long hours, particularly for live-in caregivers, and unreasonable completion of tasks, and physical and emotional abuse from some employers and the people they provide care. Eighty percent are women. The median age is 44 years. Ninety percent of them were born in the Philippines and an overwhelming 35 per-cent came into the U.S. only in the past ten years. Sixty percent have U.S. citizenship. Their median annual income was $17,050 in 2005. About 35 percent of them worked only part time and 15 percent worked overtime. About a third have at least a college-level degree and another 30 percent attended college without completion. Surprisingly three percent have graduate and post-BA level degrees.

Filipino airport workers organizing for jobs and justice in northern California as the result of the September 11, 2001 scapegoating.

AIRPORT WORKERS Filipino men and women who worked at public airports—particularly in West Coast—as screeners and baggage handlers have faced discrimination due to English language ability, age, and national origins after September 11, 2001. Airport workers include those who work as baggage and cargo handlers, fuel workers, mechanics, ticket readers, and cabin cleaners. Filipino and many non-Whites and non-U.S. citizens lost their jobs due to racial and xenophobic scapegoating. Filipino screeners faced undue burden to regain their jobs. They needed to gain U.S. citizenship (if they were holding Philippine citizenship) and pass biased hiring tests on the English language and computer skills. While they were highly experienced in doing their jobs, many did not pass the hiring tests. Nevertheless, some have been able to get their jobs back at the airports. Many others have sought employment in home care and in private security companies. A good number remained unemployed.

Table 10. Occupational Concentration for Managerial and High-Income Professional Occupations, By Gender and Census Regions

MEN	USA		Los Angeles, Riverside, Orange Cnty CA		SF, SJ, Oakland, CA		Honolulu, HI region		NYC, N. NJ, Long Island, NY, CT, PA	
	% Filipinos	% All	% Filipinos	% All	% Filipinos	% All	% Filipinos	% All	% Filipinos	% All
TOTAL	52.5*	46.7	60.7*	47.9	54.6	57.2	30.2	47.5	66.7*	52.5
Lower-Level Professionals										
Community & social services occupations	0.8	1.1	0.9	1.0	0.7	0.9	0.7	1.2	0.9	1.1
Education, training, & library occupations	1.5	2.8	1.5	2.9	1.1	2.7	1.5	3.5	1.3	3.1
Top sales & related occupations	4.4	5.4	4.9	5.7	4.8	5.3	3.8	5.1	4.5	5.9
Office & administrative support occupations	14.6*	7.2	17.9*	8.5	18.0*	7.7	9.0*	8.6	15.4*	8.6
Middle-Level Professionals										
Drafters & mapping technicians	1.6*	0.9	2.0*	0.7	2.2*	1.0	1.0*	0.9	1.1*	0.6
Life, physical and social sciences occupations	1.0	1.0	1.0*	0.8	1.1	1.7	0.2	1.1	1.4*	1.1
Arts, design, entertainment, sports, & media occupations	2.0*	1.9	2.7	3.5	1.8	2.7	1.6	2.5	2.5	3.0
Registered nurses, therapists & other health diagnosing & treating practitioners & technical occupations	3.1*	1.0	3.3*	1.0	1.4*	0.9	0.7	1.3	6.6*	1.1
Health technologists & technicians	2.1*	0.5	3.1*	0.6	1.6*	0.5	0.9*	0.8	3.9*	0.6
Supervisors, construction & extraction workers	0.4	1.3	0.3	1.0	0.4	1.1	0.9	1.0	0.2	1.0
Supervisors, transportation & material moving workers	0.2	0.3	0.2	0.3	0.2	0.2	0.3	0.3	0.2	0.3
Top Executives and Professionals										
Management occupations, except farmers & farm managers	5.6	10.0	6.5	10.6	5.7	13.2	4.1	9.8	6.4	11.7
Farmers & farm managers	0.1	1.0	0.0	0.1	0.0	0.2	0.3	0.4	0.0	0.1
Business operations specialists	1.8	1.8	2.1*	1.9	2.0	2.4	1.0	1.8	2.1	2.1
Financial specialists	2.8*	1.9	4.4*	2.0	2.8*	2.3	1.2	2.3	4.5*	3.1
Computer & mathematical occupations	4.9*	3.2	4.2*	2.8	6.0	7.4	1.2	2.3	8.1*	4.1
Architects, surveyors, cartographers, and engineers	3.3*	2.5	4.1*	2.6	4.0	4.7	1.0	2.2	3.2*	2.0
Doctors & surgeons	1.8*	0.7	0.8*	0.7	0.2	0.8	0.3	1.0	3.4*	1.1
Legal	0.5	1.1	0.7	1.2	0.5	1.5	0.3	1.3	0.8	1.9

Note: A "*" symbol indicates overrepresentation compared to the general population. *(Con't Next Page)*
Source: U.S. Census 2000 SF-4 (Tables QT-P28)

SEAFARERS There are tens of thousands of active Filipino seafarers working for U.S. transport ships, offshore drilling, and other maritime environments. Seafarers work on container ships, bulk carriers, dry cargo ships, tankers, supply ships, offshore installations, merchant ships, and oil-drilling platforms. Shipboard positions include wiper, oiler, cook, mess person, crane operator, electrician, oil/motor-person, galley helper, cable handler, handy person, mechanics, boat driver, repairperson, technicians, bosun, deck cadet, engine cadet, mate, engineer, lineman, stockperson, construction crew, diving support, ballast operators, welders, riggers, floorhand, and roustabout.

MEN	San Diego, CA region		Chicago, IL-Gary, IN-Kenosha, WI		Seattle, Tacoma, Bremerton, WA		Washington, DC-Baltimore, MD, VA, WV		Las Vegas, NV, AZ region		Sacramento-Yolo, CA region	
	% Filipinos	% All	% Filipinos	% All	% Filipinos	% All	% Filipinos	% All	% Filipinos	% All	% Filipinos	% All
TOTAL	**49.5**	**51.8**	**62.5***	**48.4**	**46.4**	**51.7**	**68.0***	**58.4**	**32.2**	**36.0**	**54.0***	**51.0**
Lower-Level Professional Workers												
Community & social services occupations	0.8	1.0	0.8	1.0	0.6	1.2	0.4	1.1	0.5	0.5	1.2	1.2
Education, training & library occupations	1.7	3.1	0.9	2.6	1.2	2.6	1.9	2.9	0.4	1.7	1.7	3.2
Top sales & related occupations	3.9	5.7	4.0	5.7	3.8	5.5	4.6	4.7	5.5*	5.1	4.4	5.7
Office & administrative support occupations	16.7*	7.8	16.6*	8.2	15.6*	7.5	14.5*	7.7	12.7*	7.1	18.0*	8.8
Middle-Level Professional Workers												
Drafters & mapping technicians	2.3*	1.1	1.8*	0.7	1.6*	1.0	1.5*	0.8	0.7	0.7	1.3*	0.8
Life, physical and social sciences occupations	1.1	1.7	1.4*	0.9	0.6	1.1	1.8	2.2	0.3	0.5	0.7	1.2
Arts, design, entertainment, sports, & media occupations	1.9	2.4	1.7	1.9	1.6	2.2	2.5	2.6	1.6	2.1	1.2	1.8
Registered nurses, therapists & other health diagnosing & treating practitioners & technical occupations	1.3*	1.1	6.4*	0.9	0.8	1.1	2.7*	0.9	1.3*	0.8	2.2*	1.2
Health technologists & technicians	2.3*	0.7	2.7*	0.4	1.8*	0.6	2.1*	0.5	0.9*	0.6	1.4*	0.6
Supervisors, construction & extraction workers	0.2	1.3	0.1	0.8	0.1	1.2	0.1	1.2	0.0	1.7	0.2	1.2
Supervisors, transportation & material moving workers	0.1	0.2	0.2	0.3	0.4	0.3	0.1	0.3	0.1	0.3	0.1	0.3
Top Executives and Professionals												
Management occupations, except farmers & farm managers	5.0	11.3	5.2	11.4	5.5	11.6	7.8	12.8	2.4	8.3	5.3	10.5
Farmers & farm managers	0.0	0.2	0.0	0.1	0	0.2	0.0	0.2	0.0	0.1	0.0	0.3
Business operations specialists	2.0	2.2	1.9	2.3	1.5	2.2	2.9	3.0	1.2	1.3	1.9	2.3
Financial specialists	2.1*	1.9	3.3*	2.4	2.3*	2.0	3.9*	2.8	1.4*	1.3	3.2*	2.1
Computer & mathematical occupations	4.0	4.2	6.9*	3.9	5.3	5.7	12.6*	7.7	1.1	1.4	6.0*	4.4
Architects, surveyors, cartographers, and engineers	3.0	3.5	4.1*	2.5	3.2	4.0	4.2*	3.3	1.4*	1.2	3.9*	3.1
Doctors and surgeons	0.4	0.8	3.0*	0.8	0.2	0.7	2.6*	0.9	0.6*	0.5	0.7	0.7
Legal	0.3	1.3	1.0	1.5	0.2	1.1	1.6	2.7	0.2	0.8	0.7	1.4

Note: A "*" symbol indicates overrepresentation compared to the general population.
Source: U.S. Census 2000 SF-4 (Tables QT-P28)

(Con't Next Page)

A quarter of the seafarers in the world are disproportionately Filipinos, some are employed and many others, about two thirds, are unemployed waiting for jobs. Firms hire Filipinos—mostly men—as seafarers because of their English language ability, labor skills, and willingness to work in harsh conditions. They hold short time contracts, face difficult workplace conditions—such as isolation and remoteness, job hazards and occupational injuries, transient quality of life, and very limited communication with family members—, and have very limited employment protection. They have long hours, often without being paid, delayed payment of wages, and

WOMEN	USA		Los Angeles, Riverside, Orange Cnty CA		SF, SJ, Oakland, CA		Honolulu, HI region		NYC, N. NJ, Long Island, NY, CT, PA	
	% Filipinos	% All	% Filipinos	% All	% Filipinos	% All	% Filipinos	% All	% Filipinos	% All
TOTAL	**68.3**	**66.9**	**76.3***	**67.2**	**69.7**	**73.0**	**54.9**	**68.0**	**81.1***	**71.7**
Lower-Level Professional Workers										
Community & social services occupations	1.0*	0.8	1.1*	0.8	1.1	1.7	1.2	2.0	1.4*	1.1
Education, training & library occupations	3.6	8.9	3.8	8.7	2.7	7.9	4.7	9.2	3.4	9.8
Top sales & related occupations	5.4	6.0	4.5	6.2	5.1	5.5	8.4*	7.4	3.7	5.4
Office & administrative support occupations	22.6	24.8	26.3*	25.0	28.0*	23.2	23.7	25.0	17.8	25.4
Middle-Level Professional Workers										
Drafters & mapping technicians	0.4*	0.2	0.4*	0.2	0.6*	0.4	0.1	0.2	0.1	0.1
Life, physical and social sciences occupations	1.0*	0.8	1.1*	0.8	1.1	1.7	0.3	0.7	1.4*	1.1
Arts, design, entertainment, sports, & media occupations	1.2	1.9	1.2	2.8	1.0	3.1	1.0	1.9	1.7	3.0
Registered nurses, therapists & other health diagnosing & treating practitioners & technical occupations	13.5*	4.5	15.0*	3.6	7.2*	3.8	3.2	4.1	29.4*	5.0
Health technologists & technicians	3.8*	2.4	5.1*	1.7	3.3*	1.6	2.4	1.7	4.2*	1.9
Supervisors, construction & extraction workers	0.0	0.0	0.0	0.0	0.0	0.0	0.0	0.0	0.0	0.0
Supervisors, transportation & material moving workers	0.0	0.1	0.0	0.1	0.1	0.1	0.2	0.1	0.0	0.1
Top Executives and Professionals										
Management occupations, except farmers & farm managers	5.1	6.9	5.7	7.8	6.7	10.5	3.7	7.0	5.6	8.0
Farmers & farm managers	0.1	0.2	0.0	0.0	0.0	0.1	0.2	0.2	0.0	0.0
Business operations specialists	2.2	2.4	2.5	2.5	3.1	3.6	1.5	2.1	1.8	2.6
Financial specialists	4.2*	2.5	6.3*	2.8	5.1*	3.4	2.9	3.2	4.6*	2.7
Computer & mathematical occupations	1.9*	1.6	1.6*	1.3	2.5	3.2	0.6	1.1	3.2*	1.9
Architects, surveyors, cartographers, and engineers	0.5*	0.4	0.5*	0.4	0.9	1.0	0.2	0.4	0.3	0.3
Doctors and surgeons	1.1*	0.3	0.6*	0.3	0.2	0.4	0.2	0.3	2.3*	0.5
Legal occupations	0.7	1.1	0.7	1.3	0.9	1.7	0.5	1.2	0.8	1.6

Note: A "*" symbol indicates overrepresentation compared to the general population.
Source: U.S. Census 2000 SF-4 (Tables QT-P28)

(Con't Next Page)

prevention of future hiring if the seafarer seeks work improvements. Challenges in U.S. courts are beginning to make U.S. firms take responsibility for work conditions and labor contract enforcement. Seafarers who "jump" ship lack accepted work and resident documentation and have no record of passing through a port of entry, thereby complicating attempts to regularize their work and resident status.

What is the social portrait and condition of U.S. Filipino professionals?

About 1.7 million—around 35 percent to 45 percent—U.S. Filipinos hold middle income and professional jobs. Yet they continually face economic instability. Many of them hold jobs such as: registered nurses (7.66 percent of U.S. Filipinos), accountants and auditors (3.10 percent), administrative assistants (1.95 percent), other-clas-

WOMEN	San Diego, CA region		Chicago, IL-Gary, IN-Kenosha, WI		Seattle, Tacoma, Bremerton, WA		Washington, DC-Baltimore, MD, VA, WV		Las Vegas, NV, AZ region		Sacramento-Yolo, CA region	
	% Filipinos	% All	% Filipinos	% All	% Filipinos	% All	% Filipinos	% All	% Filipinos	% All	% Filipinos	% All
TOTAL	**64.0**	**69.0**	**79.5***	**70.6**	**61.2**	**69.9**	**68.8**	**75.8**	**51.7**	**59.8**	**71.7**	**72.7**
Lower-Level Professional Workers												
Community & social services occupations	1.2	1.9	0.7	1.8	0.6	1.0	0.7	2.1	0.3	1.0	2.4	2.2
Education, training & library occupations	3.7	8.8	2.9	8.6	2.7	7.8	3.0	8.7	1.7	6.0	3.6	8.5
Top sales & related occupations	5.3	6.3	3.8	6.1	5.6	5.9	4.5	5.0	9.6*	7.8	4.1	5.3
Office & administrative support occupations	23.9	23.9	18.9	26.4	23.3	23.9	22.0	24.1	19.5	25.1	27.4*	27.3
Middle-Level Professional Workers												
Drafters & mapping technicians	1.0	0.3	0.2	0.2	0.4*	0.3	0.1	0.2	0.2	0.1	0.7*	0.2
Life, physical & social sciences occupations	1.3	1.5	1.3*	0.9	0.6	1.0	1.5	1.7	0.1	0.3	1.2*	1.1
Arts, design, entertainment, sports, & media occupations	0.9	2.4	1.0	2.1	1.3	2.6	1.8	2.9	0.7	1.9	1.0	1.9
Registered nurses, therapists & other health diagnosing & treating practitioners & technical occupations	9.8*	4.0	28.5*	4.6	7.0*	4.3	10.6*	4.2	8.5*	3.1	9.4*	3.9
Health technologists & technicians	4.3*	2.0	4.7*	2.0	3.7*	2.0	3.0*	1.9	2.6*	1.7	3.2*	1.8
Supervisors, construction & extraction workers	0.0	0.0	0.0	0.0	0.1	0.1	0.0	0.0	0.0	0.1	0.0	0.1
Supervisors, transportation & material moving workers	0.0	0.0	0.0	0.1	0.1	0.1	0.1	0.1	0.0	0.1	0.0	0.0
Top Executives and Professionals												
Management occupations, except farmers & farm managers	4.1	8.3	5.1	7.9	4.9	8.6	6.1	9.9	2.4	6.5	4.8	8.0
Farmers & farm managers	0.0	0.1	0.0	0.0	0.1	0.1	0.0	0.1	0.0	0.0	0.2	0.1
Business operations specialists	1.9	2.8	1.6	3.0	2.7	3.2	2.5	4.1	1.5	1.9	3.3	3.5
Financial specialists	4.0*	2.8	4.9*	2.8	4.0*	2.9	5.2*	3.3	3.0*	2.1	4.7*	3.3
Computer & mathematical occupations	1.1	1.7	2.5*	2.0	1.4	2.5	4.0	4.2	0.2	0.7	4.5*	3.2
Architects, surveyors, cartographers, and engineers	0.6*	0.5	0.6	0.4	0.8*	0.7	0.6	0.5	0.5*	0.2	0.5	0.6
Doctors and surgeons	0.2	0.3	1.9*	0.4	0.4	0.4	1.8*	0.5	0.3*	0.2	0.2	0.3
Legal occupations	0.6	1.4	0.8	1.2	0.9	1.5	1.2	2.3	0.6	1.1	0.7	1.6

Note: A "*" symbol indicates overrepresentation compared to the general population.
Source: U.S. Census 2000 SF-4 (Tables QT-P28)

sified managers (1.42 percent), physicians and surgeons (1.37 percent), bookkeeping, accounting, and auditing clerks (1.36 percent), retail sales supervisors (1.31 percent), administrative support worker supervisors (1.15 percent), elementary and middle school teachers (1.08 percent), and clinical laboratory technologists and technicians (1.08 percent). Moreover, about 14 percent of U.S. Filipinos are employed in the federal, state, or local government. In addition, three percent of U.S. Filipinos are small business owners, less than typical for groups in the U.S. Table 10 provides additional details on regional variations involving U.S. Filipino professionals.

Sixty percent of U.S. Filipinos live in their own homes, as compared to 67 percent for the general population. The me-

Table 11. Lower-Middle Income U.S. Filipino Communities, By U.S. States

U.S. State	Areas With Mostly Lower-Middle With Some Low Income	Lower-Middle Income Areas
California	168	164
New Jersey	10	16
Illinois	6	11
Virginia	3	5
New York	10	3
Hawaii	21	2
Texas	2	2
Maryland	1	2
Florida	2	1
Washington	2	1
Nevada	1	0
Total	**226**	**207**
% Service Workers	18.6	10.0
Average Earnings ($)	18,000	23,000

Source: U.S. Census 2000, National Bulosan Center Research

dian monthly housing cost with a mortgage for U.S. Filipino homeowners is $1,922, as compared to $1,295 for the general population. The average household size for these homes is 3.5 for U.S. Filipinos, as compared to 2.7 for the general population. The average occupant per room in an owner-occupied unit is 0.85 for Filipinos compared to 0.59 for the general population. In addition, thirty-eight percent of U.S. Filipino homeowners spend 30 percent or more of household income on housing.

COMMUNITIES IN FLUX Middle-income and professional Filipinos live and work in many U.S. urban and suburban areas.

Often they reside in communities without a strong Filipino presence; some nevertheless continue to live among Filipino workers. A good number live in white homogenous neighborhoods while some reside and work in variant multiracial and multi-ethnic communities.

As discussed earlier, a portion of middle-income and professional Filipinos reside in areas with some low income Filipinos. In addition, a significant number reside in lower-middle areas. On average, these mixed-income and lower middle-income areas comprise of 12 percent of Filipinos living in rental units, 10.0 percent of Filipinos working in low-income service and clerical related occupations, 13.9 percent of Filipinos working in professional occupations, and 6.9 percent of Filipinos working in production related occupations. Filipinos living in a typical lower-middle income area earned on average about $23,000 in 1999. In contrast, Filipinos living in middle income areas earned on average about $54,300.

Table 11 highlights the lower-middle income character of many areas in California and across the U.S., primarily present in New Jersey, Illinois, and Virginia. This pattern reflects the steady recruitment from the Philippines of Filipino nurses and other health care professionals into these urban areas.

SOCIAL CONDITIONS Middle-income and professional Filipinos face many issues similar to low-income and semi-skilled Filipinos. They deal with issues of anti-Filipino economic injustice, racism and bogus assimilation and an unjust legal system, and family separation. In addition, they experience **economic underemployment and job deskilling**. Compared to other groups,

U.S. Filipino educators protest for their rights.

middle-class Filipinos trained in the Philippines continue to find work at lower occupational level relative to their formal education training (i.e. teachers, nurses, doctors, engineers, and so on). They tend to work in jobs with lower pay and benefits and little opportunities for advancement (i.e. high-end service jobs or low-end technical skills jobs). Forty-eight percent of U.S. Filipinas have a bachelor degree or higher, compared with only 26 percent of women in the general U.S. population. Similarly, forty-one percent of U.S. Filipino men have a bachelor degree or higher, compared with only 29 percent of general male population. Moreover, middle-class Filipinos face difficulty in **maintaining home ownership** (i.e. paying the monthly mortgage and property taxes to own a home). Compared to others, middle class Filipinos get fix income, send remittances back to the Philippines, accrue and pay high personal debt (for educational expenses for their children, cars, and so on), and pay for basic needs. All these factors make it highly difficult for the middle class to own a home and forces them to seek work outside the region and move to a more relatively affordable area.

THE CASE OF TEACHERS AND OTHER EDUCATORS There are 19,800 Filipinas and Filipino men employed in educational professions across the U.S. Filipinos are underrepresented in educational professions. They tend to experience greater racial harassment—including physical violence—from students, parents, and other staff members. They work with limited resources to do their job adequately.

U.S. Filipino health care workers and professionals volunteering for the community.

The successful campaign for the Sentosa 27+ nurses.

Recently, there is a noticeable increase in short-term labor recruitment of teachers, via H1-B visas, from the Philippines to help resolve the public education crisis in the U.S., particularly for school districts in urban, suburban, and rural neighborhoods such as in Baltimore (MD) and New Orleans (LA). Some teachers who are trafficked by Philippine-based recruitment agencies arrived in the U.S. and found that the jobs promised do not exist. Yet the agencies got paid by school districts and by the trafficked teachers.

Seventy-five percent of them are women. The median age is 38 years. Two thirds of them were born in the Philippines and 30 percent came into the U.S. only in the past ten years. Seventy-three percent of them have U.S. citizenship. Their median annual income was $30,000 in 2005. Fifteen percent of them worked overtime.

What are the specific issues of U.S. Filipinos employed across multiple occupations in selected industries?

HEALTH CARE WORKERS AND PROFESSIONALS There are 686,000 Filipinas and Filipino men employed as health workers and professionals. They are overrepresented in the healthcare industry. They are employed as registered nurses, therapists, nursing, psychiatric, and home health aides, occupational and physical therapist assistants and aides, health technologists and technicians, other health diagnosing and treating practitioners, pharmacists, dentists, and physicians and surgeons.

Filipinas tend to be overrepresented in these occupations compared to other groups due to labor recruitment practices. A number of Filipino men and women are hired with short-term labor contracts via H1-B visas from the Philippines and through other countries such as U.K. and Saudi Arabia. While the pay and benefits for professional Filipinas and Filipino men may be seen as higher, they tend to be targeted to work during less desirable shifts and higher levels of induced stress.

Seventy-seven percent of health care professionals are women. The median age is 44 years. Ninety percent of these

U.S. Filipino musicians promote social justice through creativity and entertainment.

professionals were born in the Philippines and an overwhelming 20 percent came into the U.S. only in the past ten years. Seventy-three percent of them have U.S. citizenship. Their median annual income was $60,000 in 2005. About 25 percent of them worked only part time and 20 percent worked overtime.

Additional studies need to examine illegal recruitment companies, what percent are hired through recruitment agencies, what is their visa status, and what percent return to the Philippines after their contract expired.

CULTURAL WORKERS AND MEDIA PROFESSIONALS There are 17,400 U.S. Filipinas and Filipino men employed as artists, journalists, designers, performers, and as other cultural workers. Filipinos are underrepresented in top managerial, executive, producer, and creative positions in the U.S. cultural industries. Due to racism, they often are not promoted and experienced barriers such as the "glass ceiling" for jobs such as writers and producers. They generally lack resources to produce their work such as studio time and money for equipment.

Many more engage in cultural activity as their life passion and yet they do not primarily work in the cultural industries. Family members tend not to support career interests of younger cultural workers, directing them to more technical and professional office careers. Those who are self-employed lack health and other benefits and often need to work in service jobs.

Fifty-four percent of them are men. The median age is 38 years. Fifty-five percent of them were born in the U.S. Of those born in the Philippines, 21 percent came into the U.S. only in the past ten years. Eighty-five percent of them have U.S. citizenship. Their median annual income was $28,000 in 2005. Sixty-three percent of them 25 years and over have at least a college-level degree.

What is the social portrait and condition of U.S. Filipinos who are owners of small and medium-size businesses?

Small business owners operate firms locally, often consisting of the self-employed owner and up to ten employees. These firms' annual revenue rarely exceeds one million dollars. These owners tend to operate, for instance, real estate and insurance franchise, restaurants, retail outlets, wholesale trade, and health services. Some are independent contractors.

Middle-size business owners operate firms with U.S. national and international reach, often with business capital assets up to $250 million. Examples include Loida Nicolas Lewis of TLC Beatrice, Lilla and Leopoldo Clementa of Clementa Capital, a

Table 12. U.S. Filipino Businesses, By Industry Groups and By Economic Census Areas

Industry Groups	Number of Firms	Sales ($1000)	Number of Employees	Payroll ($1000)
Agricultural services, forestry & fishing	113	19,661	281	5,342
Construction industries and subdividers & developers	79	110,143	545	15,219
Manufacturing	435	887,035	5,379	144,629
Wholesale trade	1,107	1,967,219	5,723	157,888
Retail trade	1,555	569,746	9,210	87,927
Finance, insurance & real estate industries	370	203,151	2,186	49,391
Service industries	9,626	4,323,873	75,646	1,948,170
Business services	513	230,900	4,490	115,283
Health services	6,504	3,446,950	58,837	1,610,830
Social services	646	202,116	4,833	70,465
ALL INDUSTRIES	**14,581**	**8,966,386**	**110,130**	**2,667,333**

Economic Census Areas (including surrounding areas)	Percent Business Filipino Owners in the Area	Number of Firms	Sales ($1000)	Number of Employees	Payroll ($1000)
Los Angeles & Long Beach, CA region	1.2%	1,473	1,533,699	28,280	658,807
Riverside, CA region		99	105,833	941	22,654
Oakland, CA region		551	193,764	2,482	42,567
San Francisco, CA region	0.5%	405	225,895	3,070	52,978
San Jose, CA region		143	116,225	1,326	40,061
Honolulu, CA region	0.6%	663	275,702	3,449	70,541
Jersey City, NJ region		129	145,477	91	8,954
Middlesex, Somerset, Hunterdon, NJ region		132	234,339	2,796	88,443
New York City, NY region	1.0%	745	697,419	7,932	246,670
San Diego, CA region	0.4%	753	289,149	3,271	51,529
Chicago, IL area	1.1%	508	440,606	2,732	94,764
Gary, IN area		44	D	100 to 249	D
Kenosha, WI area		6	D	20 to 99	D
Seattle, Bellevue, Everett, WA region	0.5%	156	118,979	730	17,319
Washington, DC, MD, VA, WV area	0.8%	267	148, 497	2,201	66,666
Baltimore, MD area		169	56,509	546	15,195
Hagerstown, MD area		29	D	100 to 249	D
Las Vegas, NV-AZ region	0.4%	86	24,302	479	7,939
Sacramento, CA area	0.5%	133	67,216	1,526	22,676

Note: Firm census information combines big business and transnational business owners. A "D" symbol indicates information withheld to avoid disclosure of detailed firm data. Source: U.S. Economic Census 1997, U.S. Census 2000 SF-4 (Table QT-P25)

Table 13. U.S. Filipino Small and Medium-Size Business Owners by Gender and U.S. Census Regions

Self-Employed	Men		Women	
	% Filipinos	% All	% Filipinos	% All
Regions				
Los Angeles, Riverside, Orange Cnty CA	4.5	9.5	3.5	7.0
SF, SJ, Oakland, CA	3.7	8.8	2.8	7.6
Honolulu, HI region	3.5	7.0	3.0	5.5
NYC, N. NJ, Long Island, NY, CT, PA	3.3	6.8	3.5	4.4
San Diego, CA region	3.3	9.4	2.5	7.8
Chicago, IL-Gary, IN-Kenosha, WI	3.3	5.1	3.0	3.9
Seattle, Tacoma, Bremerton, WA	3.0	6.9	4.5	6.3
Washington, DC-Baltimore, MD, VA, WV region	3.3	5.6	5.4*	4.8
Las Vegas, NV, AZ region	1.9	4.8	2.8	4.1
Sacramento-Yolo, CA region	3.2	8.9	3.2	6.6
U.S.A.	3.7	7.8	3.1	5.3

Note: A "*" symbol indicates overrepresentation compared to the general population. Source: U.S. Census 2000 SF-4 (Table QT-P25)

global fund management firm, Diosdado Banatao, a venture capitalist and engineer with a reported net worth of $100 million and Josie Natori of the Natori Company with annual net revenue of $50 million.

There are about 80,000 to 160,000 Filipino business owners in the U.S., about 2-4 percent of U.S. Filipinos. Fifty-six percent of them are disproportionately men. Eighty-three percent of them have U.S. citizenship. Seventy-eight percent of them were born in the Philippines. Over half of them came before 1981: only ten percent came into the U.S. only in the past ten years. Sixty-four percent of them have at least a bachelor college degree for those 25 years and over. The reported median annual income for Filipino business owners in the U.S. was $75,000 in 2005.

Over 42 percent of affluent Filipinos reside in California (in places such as parts of Solano, San Mateo, southern Alameda, Los Angeles, and San Diego counties). Another 11 percent live in Connecticut. Many of other affluent reside in Illinois (9 percent), Texas (9 percent), New Jersey (5 percent), and New York (5 percent).

Filipino-owned businesses in the U.S. employ over 132,000 workers and earn nearly $14.2 billion in revenue annually. Around 40 percent of Filipino-owned firms operate in health care and social assistance sector, one percent in professional, scientific and technical services sector. These businesses are primarily concentrated in California, Hawai'i, New York, Illinois, New York, Florida, and Texas.

Jollibee provides orientations to potential employees in the U.S.

Table 12 highlights the characteristics of their business operations of small and medium-size business owners. Table 13 profiles their regional variation.

What is the social portrait of U.S. Filipinos who are transnational land and business owners in the Philippines?

This class consists of the immediate family members of the top Philippine business and property conglomerates who reside in the U.S. and their owners, head executives, and lawyers when they stay and conduct business in the U.S. These prominent wealthy families have close intimate ties with the U.S. economic and political structure and seek to influence U.S. political and economic relations with the Philippines. Some of them start business ventures in the U.S. to provide products and services primarily directed to Filipinos in the U.S. There are less than 40,000—less than one percent of total—U.S. Filipinos who are members of this class.

For instance, Mona Lisa Yuchengo, who publishes U.S.-based *Filipinas* magazine and runs an international charity, is the daughter of Alfonso Yuchengo, who heads the Yuchengco Group of Companies in banking, education, construction, and education in the Philippines, an ambassador for the Philippine government, and with net worth of $365 million.

Major Philippine conglomerates have been expanding their operations into the U.S. Examples of these operations include Philippine Airlines and Philippine National Bank (of the Lucio Tan family with net worth of $1.6 billion), Bank of the Philippines, property firms, and Ayala Foundation (of the Zobel de Ayala family), San Miguel beer and property firms (of the Cojuangco family), ABS-CBN Broadcasting (of the Oscar Lopez family with net worth of $775 million), GMA media and INQ7 network (of the Gozon and Duavit families), and Jollibee Foods (of the Tony Tan Caktiong family with net worth of $760 million).

In addition, sons and daughters of top property and business owners of the Philippines often attend prestigious universities in the U.S. For instance, the daughter of former Philippine President Diosdado Macapagal and current President, Gloria Macapagal-Arroyo, earned her A.B. in Economics from Georgetown University, Washington, D.C. in 1964-1966. While attending college in the U.S., she sought to build strong ties with classmates who might become national and global leaders and business executives such as future U.S. President William "Bill" Clinton.

4 Social Groups Among U.S. Filipinos

What are the major social groups among Filipinos in the U.S.?

Several social groups among U.S. Filipinos face unique concerns, challenges, and prospects (see Table 14). These groups include:

1. Migrants (including contract workers, immigrants, and undocumented people)
2. Descendants
3. Women
4. Lesbians, gay men, bisexuals, and transgender people
5. Youth and students
6. Seniors
7. People with disability
8. Religious groups (including Catholics and the Bangsa Moro people)
9. Philippine national minorities
10. Government workers and professionals
11. Military personnel and war veterans
12. Mainstream politicians
13. Non-traditional earners
14. People living in the margins of society.

It is important to give attention to these social groups because they have their own particular needs. These groups cut across economic classes and are not outside of the economic classes in U.S. society.

Migrant Sector Members

- Temporary contract workers including seafarers
- Philippine-born U.S. residents including those who are defined by the U.S. as permanent residents ("greencard" holders) & those not allowed to live in the U.S. (i.e. the "undocumented")
- People illegally "trafficked" into the U.S.
- Filipinos who are naturalized U.S. citizens
- Children of Filipinos born outside the U.S.

What is the social portrait and condition of U.S. Filipino migrants?

U.S. Filipino migrants are comprise of those who are from the Philippines and are residing and working in the U.S. as (1) temporary contract workers, (2) authorized immigrants, and (3) unauthorized and undocumented residents.

Two-thirds of Filipinos living in the U.S.—around 2.7 million—migrated from

Table 14. Social Group Profile of U.S. Filipinos

Social Groups[1]	U.S. Filipinos	Total U.S. Population
Migrants	67%	12%
Descendants	33%	
Women	54%	51%
Lesbians, gay men, bisexuals, & transgender people	8-12%	
Youth and students	50%	
Seniors	8%	12%
People living with disability	9%	
Religious groups		
Catholics	80-85%	
The Bangsa Moro people	3-5%	
Philippine national minorities	10-15%	
Government workers and professionals	14%	12%
Military personnel and veterans	7-9%	13%
Traditional politicians	less than 1%	
Non-traditional earners	5-8%	3-5%
People living on the margins of society	3-4%	1-2%

Note: (1) See the main document for explanation of these groups. Source: U.S. Census 2006 American Community Survey, National Bulosan Center Research

the Philippines. Labor recruitment tends to favor females: sixty percent of Filipino migrants are women. They **tend to be older** than the U.S. born Filipinos: the median age of migrants is 45 years compared to 16 years for those born in the US. Only 7.2 percent of Filipino migrants are under 18, compared with 15 percent of people 65 years old and over. Fifty percent of them have at least a bachelor college degree for those 25 years and over. The other 26 percent earned at least a high school degree.

Around 75,000 new Filipinos officially arrived in 2006, as reported by the U.S. Homeland Security Department: about 4,100 temporary contract workers came

from the Philippines in 2005, as reported by the Philippine Overseas Employment Administration. The majority of them came from a peasant or worker background in the Philippines. Some of them came from the professional class in the Philippines. They often do not intend to stay here, but are forced to remain in the U.S. due to conditions in the Philippines, separating families and transforming family relations.

In 2005, over 60 percent of global remittances into the Philippine economy came from the U.S. (US$5.32 billion out of US$8.83 billion).

During the past decade, twenty-six percent came into the U.S. Thirty percent came during the period 1986 to 1995. There was a slight decrease in entry from 1996 to 2000. Only four percent came before 1965. Moreover, 64 percent of migrants have U.S. citizenship.

Recently, a significant majority entered through family sponsorship—such as spouses, children, parents, and others—while only 27 percent entered through employment sponsorship. Fifty percent of contract migrants arrived using H1-B visas for specialty occupations while only one percent use H1-A and H1-C visas to work as registered nurses.

Tables 15, 16, 17, 18, 19, 20, 21, 22, 23, 24, 25, and 26 provide additional information on U.S. Filipino migrants.

CONTRACT MIGRANTS The experiences of these temporary workers are shaped by their conditions of employment, wage, housing, mobility, and termination. They are recruited to work as registered nurses, teachers, service workers in the entertainment industry, programmers, and developers for the information technology industry, and professional artists. They are often unclear about their actual employment rights: they do not want to make a fuss for fear of retaliation. They are expected to pay for recruitment fees, early termination fees, and other hidden fees. At times, seemingly valid and legal contracts become instruments for illegal recruitment.

Other temporary migrants include tourists, visitors, performers, trainees, and religious workers. (See Tables 18 and 19 for limited information.) Once in the U.S., some of these temporary migrants overstay their visa and become unauthorized.

More research is needed on the adherence to U.S. labor laws in the

Table 15. Authorized Filipino Migration to the U.S., By Period of Entry

Period	Filipinos[1]	% of Total Migrants	% of Total Filipino Migrants
1930-1939	391	0.1	0.0
1940-1949	4,099	0.5	0.2
1950-1959	17,245	0.7	0.9
1960-1969	70,660	2.2	3.9
1970-1979	337,726	7.9	18.4
1980-1989	502,056	8.0	27.4
1990-1999	534,338	5.5	29.2
2000-2006	366,176	5.2	20.0
1930-2006	1,832,691	5.3	100.0

Note: (1) This is official U.S. Department of Homeland Security tally, which does not include undocumented residence and people who are not officially counted.
Source: U.S. Department of Homeland Security 2006 (Table 2)

Table 16. Reasons for Authorized Filipino Immigration to the U.S.

Admission Reason	% Filipino Admitted, 2004	% Filipino Admitted, 2006	% Total Admitted, 2006
Immediate relatives of U.S. citizens	42.7	46.0	5.9
Employment-based preferences	26.8	31.8	14.9
Family-sponsored preferences	30.1	21.5	7.2
Refugees and asylum-granted	0.1	0.4	7.5
Other	0.3	0.3	0.1
Diversity	0.0	0.0	0.0

Source: U.S. Department of Homeland Security 2004 (Table 8) and 2006 (Table 10)

Table 17. Top U.S. Port of Entry for Temporary Migrants from the Philippines

Port of Entry	Percent of Port of Entry
Los Angeles, CA	33.2
San Francisco, CA	17.9
Agana, Guam	7.5
New York, NY	7.0

Source: U.S. Department of Homeland Security 2004 (Table 24)

contracts signed by these migrants, what happens when contracts are not renewed, and the collusion among the U.S. government, the Philippine government, and the recruitment agencies.

AUTHORIZED IMMIGRANTS The median annual income for Filipino immigrants was $25,000 in 2005, compared to $17,400 for U.S. born who tended to be much younger, to have less formal education, and to have less work experiences.

Sixty-six percent of U.S. Filipino immigrants age 16 years and over are working or seeking employment. About 70 percent of immigrants work in the for-profit sector while 8.9 percent work for nonprofits. Six percent of them work for local governments, 3.7 percent for state governments, and 6.3 for the federal government. Moreover, 3.7 percent of immigrants run their own business.

They tend to be concentrated in industries such as hospitals (15.3 percent of Filipino immigrants), hotels and motels (3.4 percent), food services (3.9 percent), elementary and secondary schools (2.4 percent), department and discount stores (2.1 percent), and banking institutions (2.0 percent). They also tend to be concentrated in occupations such as registered nurses (9.9 percent of Filipino immigrants), nursing, psychiatric, and home health aides (3.7 percent), accountants and auditors (3.7 percent), cashiers (2.9 percent), retail salespersons (2.3 percent), maids and housekeeping cleaners (2.1 percent), janitors and building cleaners

U.S. Filipinos fighting against racial discrimination and for immigration rights.

(1.7 percent), bookkeeping, accounting, and auditing clerks (1.5 percent), clinical laboratory technologists and technicians (1.4 percent), and miscellaneous managers (1.3 percent).

In the first few years, authorized immigrants face financial, cultural, and emotional hardship in their transition to live and work in the U.S. They face increased mental health issues, and some continue to promote feudal relations and values in the family. They quickly seek work, a place to live, and stability and security for their family. Over time, authorized immigrants tend to become more stable. They often seek a path to U.S. citizenship, especially to petition family members to the U.S. and to avoid paying higher citizenship application fees. Some do not want to obtain U.S. citizenship due to national pride. Some quickly become attached to newly obtained assets such as homes. Some are unsympathetic to the concerns of undocumented migrants. They participate in church and provincial associations. More research is needed on newcomer immigrant families during their first five years.

Table 18. Admission Category for Temporary Migrants From the Philippines (Total = 284,060 in 2006)

Admission Category	Percent Total Filipino Admitted
Tourists and business travelers (B-1, B-2, BCC, GB, BT, WB, and WT admission categories)	63.3
All other classes	26.7
Temporary workers (E-1 to E-3, H-1B, H-1B1, H-1C, H-2A, H-2B, H-2R, H-3, H-4, I-1, L-1, L-2, O-1 to O-3, P-1 to P-4, Q-1, R-1, R-2, TD and TN admission categories)	6.3
Students and exchange visitors (F-1 to F-3, J-1, J-2, and M-1 to M-3 admission categories)	1.7
Diplomats and other representatives (A-1 to A-3, G-1 to G-5, and N-1 to N-7 admission categories)	1.6
Unknown	0.4

Source: U.S. Department of Homeland Security 2006 (Table 29)

Table 19. Visa Category for Temporary Migrant Workers From the Philippines (Total = 17,929 in 2006)

Visa Category Admitted	Percent Total Filipino Worker
Specialty occupations (H-1B admission category)	31.9
Intracompany transferees (L1 admission category)	15.5
Nonagricultural seasonal workers (H-2B admission category)	8.1
Extraordinary ability/achievement (O1, O2 admission categories)	2.7
Athletes, artists, and entertainers (P1 to P3 admission categories)	2.0
Agricultural seasonal workers (H-2A admission category)	0.1
Treaty traders and investors (E1-E3 admission categories)	7.0
Other (H-1B1, H-1C, H-3, H-4, I-1, L-2, O-3, P-4, Q-1, R-1, R-2, TD and TN admission categories)	32.7

Source: U.S. Department of Homeland Security 2006 (Table 33)

Table 20. Top Ranked U.S. Urban Areas
Where Authorized Filipino Immigrants Reside

Urban Area	% of Area	Urban Area	% of Area
Los Angeles	12.3	San Diego, CA	4.9
Honolulu, HI	4.9	Oakland, CA	4.2
Chicago IL	4.2	San Francisco, CA	4.1
Washington, DC	3.3	San Jose, CA	3.4
New York, NY	2.9	Seattle-Bellevue-Everett, WA	2.5
Orange County, CA	2.3	Las Vegas, NV	2.1

Source: U.S. Department of Homeland Security 2003 (Table 2 Supplement)

Table 21. U.S. Filipino Born in the Philippines,
By Period of Entry and U.S. Census Region[1]

	USA		Los Angeles, Riverside, Orange Cnty CA		SF, SJ, Oakland, CA		Honolulu, HI region		NYC, N. NJ, Long Island, NY, CT, PA	
	% Filipinos	% All	% Filipinos	% All	% Filipinos	% All	% Filipinos	% All	% Filipinos	% All
Not born in the U.S.	55.8	11.1	62.7	30.9	59.6	27.0	38.2	19.2	70.0	24.4
Entered before 1980	19.8	4.7	20.9	10.8	19.3	11.0	15.0	7.5	27.9	10.0
Enter 1980-1989	18.4	3.0	23.7	10.6	20.3	8.2	10.7	5.1	24.9	6.8
Entered 1990 to Mar 2000	17.6	3.4	18.1	9.5	19.8	7.8	12.5	6.5	17.2	7.6
Not a U.S. Citizen	21.4	6.6	24.1	19.2	21.0	14.8	12.5	7.5	32.2	13.3

	San Diego, CA region		Chicago, IL-Gary, IN-Kenosha, WI		Seattle, Tacoma, Bremerton, WA		Washington, DC-Baltimore, MD, VA, WV region		Las Vegas, NV, AZ region		Sacramento-Yolo, CA region	
	% Filipinos	% All	% Filipinos	% All	% Filipinos	% All	% Filipinos	% All	% Filipinos	% All	% Filipinos	% All
Not born in the U.S.	58.3	21.5	65.7	16.0	50.7	11.7	62.3	12.9	59.5	16.5	46.2	14.5
Entered before 1980	20.0	6.8	18.5	3.8	18.4	5.3	19.7	3.7	20.5	4.6	14.2	4.1
Enter 1980-1989	19.5	7.1	23.2	5.0	15.7	2.9	18.8	3.2	15.3	4.6	16.2	4.1
Entered 1990 to Mar 2000	18.8	7.7	24.0	7.1	16.6	12.0	23.8	6.0	23.7	7.3	15.8	6.3
Not a U.S. Citizen	20.0	12.7	25.5	9.6	16.9	6.4	27.5	7.6	25.0	10.5	18.0	8.4

Note: (1) This is official U.S. census tally, which does not include undocumented residence and people who are not officially counted. Source: U.S. Census 2000 SF-4 (Tables DP-2)

Table 22. Period of Naturalization of Filipinos in the U.S.

Period	Number of Filipinos Naturalized
1991-1995	175,609
1996-2000	192,623
2001-2006	162,951

Source: U.S. Department of Homeland Security 2004 (Table 32)

Table 23. Percent Filipinos with U.S. Naturalized Citizenship, by Census Regions

	% Filipinos	% All
Census-Defined Regions		
Los Angeles, Riverside, Orange county CA	38.6	11.7
SF, SJ, Oakland, CA	38.6	12.2
Honolulu, HI region	25.7	11.7
NYC, N. NJ, Long Island, NY, CT, PA	37.8	11.1
San Diego, CA region	38.3	8.9
Chicago, IL-Gary, IN-Kenosha, WI	40.1	6.4
Seattle, Tacoma, Bremerton, WA	33.8	5.4
Washington, DC-Baltimore, MD, VA, WV region	34.7	5.3
Las Vegas, NV, AZ region	34.5	6.1
Sacramento-Yolo, CA region	28.2	6.1
U.S.A.	34.4	4.5

Source: U.S. Census 2000 SF-4 (Tables DP-2)

Table 24. Percent Filipinos with U.S. Naturalized Citizenship, by Urban Areas

Urban Area	% of Area	Urban Area	% of Area
Los Angeles	14.4	Oakland, CA	5.9
San Diego, CA	5.7	Chicago, IL	5.4
San Francisco, CA	5.1	New York, NY	4.0
San Jose, CA	3.6	Orange County, CA	3.3
Riverside, San Bernardino CA	2.8	Seattle-Bellevue-Everett, WA	2.5
Honolulu, HI	2.5	Washington DC	2.3
Las Vegas, NV	2.3		

Source: U.S. Department of Homeland Security 2003 (Table 2 Naturalization Supplement)

UNDOCUMENTED MIGRANTS While many Filipino migrants have legal residence documents, about 16 percent live in the U.S. without valid residence documents and face removal. Since September 11, 2001, thousands of U.S. Filipinos—migrant or not—are targets for deportation and inadmissibility by the Department of Homeland Security (DHS). Migrants particularly face greater scrutiny regarding their status, affecting how others threat them, including government institutions and social service agencies treat them. Under current homeland security practices, non-migrants deal with increased opportunities for removal due to DHS's regulation regarding individual conduct and activities deemed suspicious. In brief, Filipino migrants—authorized or not—continue to experience social, civic, economic, and political exclusion while living and working in the U.S. This exclusion even affects naturalized citizens and U.S.-born Filipinos due to the over-encompassing net to maintain a national security façade of order and safety.

Undocumented migrants are often paid under the table, and live with family and friends in crowded housing conditions. They live in fear of raids and deportation and fear retaliation for reporting employment abuse. They attempt to find means to adjust their status such as by seeking asylum and getting married. They become easy victims of predatory immigration schemes. They have limited access to health care and education for their children who often do not quality for college financial aid. Some fear participating in political activities due to their legal status.

Opposition to ICE raids in U.S. Filipino communities and unjust deportations of Filipinos.

Unauthorized migrant youth face challenges in school due to their English proficiency skills and restricted access to computing technology and other educational resources.

What is the social portrait of descendants of Filipino migrants in the U.S.?

Descendants of Filipino migrants comprise of a third of the U.S. Filipinos. They are born in the U.S. Some of their families have been in the U.S. for up to four generations. Many of the descendants are presently youth and students (see discussion in the section below).

Descendants tend to have strong interest in learning about family and Philip-

Table 25. Percent Filipinos with U.S. Citizenship Who Are Naturalized, By Census Region

	% Filipinos	% All
Regions		
Los Angeles, Riverside, Orange Cnty CA	37.3	69.1
SF, SJ, Oakland, CA	40.4	73.0
Honolulu, HI region	61.8	80.8
NYC, N. NJ, Long Island, NY, CT, PA	30.0	75.6
San Diego, CA region	41.7	78.5
Chicago, IL-Gary, IN-Kenosha, WI	34.3	84.0
Seattle, Tacoma, Bremerton, WA	49.3	88.3
Washington, DC-Baltimore, MD, VA, WV region	37.7	87.1
Las Vegas, NV, AZ region	40.5	83.5
Sacramento-Yolo, CA region	53.8	85.5
U.S.A.	44.2	88.9

Source: U.S. Census 2000 SF-4 (Tables DP-2)

Table 26. Philippine Overseas Absentee Voting in the U.S.

Embassy or Consulate Location	Seabased Voters	Landbased Voters	Total Voters
San Francisco, CA	6	847	853
New York, NY	9	804	813
Chicago, IL	5	688	693
Washington, DC	95	444	539
Los Angeles, CA	14	287	301
Honolulu, HI	1	117	118

Source: Philippine Commission on Elections, April 2004

Descendants of Filipino migrants in the U.S.

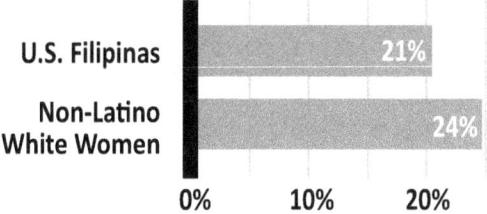

Figure 22. Percent Change In Median Full-Time Year-Round Earnings For Full-Time Year-Round Employees, 1999 and 2006. Source: 2000 U.S. Census and 2007 U.S. Census American Community Survey

pine history. They want to explore more about their social, cultural, and political identities in order to feel that they belong to a particular community. Initially they feel some separation from new Filipino migrants—due to differences in language, class experiences, and social interest—and from the mainstream of U.S. society. They focus on defining for themselves Filipino-American identity, on other aspects of social identity such as sexuality or religion, and on issues of racism, discrimination, and economic mobility.

More research is needed on the concerns of descendants who are not youth or student.

What are the social portrait and condition of U.S. Filipinas?

There are about 2.2 million Filipinas living and working in the United States, which make up 54 percent of U.S. Filipinos. The median age is 36 years. Around 24 percent of them are under 18, compared with only 10 percent of people 65 years old and over. Sixty-two percent of them were born in the Philippines: 28 percent came into the U.S. only in the past ten years. Seventy-eight percent of them have U.S. citizenship. Fifty percent of them have at least a bachelor college degree for those 25 years and over. The other 25 percent earned at least a high school degree.

U.S. Filipinas have a **higher rate of marriage**, yet they have **lower fertility rate**. Fifty-eight percent of Filipinas 15 years and over are heterosexually married, compared to 51 percent for women in the general population. Around 21 percent of Filipinas ages 15 to 50 years gave birth in the past 12 months, compared to 31 percent for women in the general population.

There are many issues confronting U.S. Filipinas presently. One of the issues involves pay and economic stability. U.S. Filipina earnings would give us one indicator of their economic situation. Earnings of Filipinas in the U.S. have grown at a slower rate—11 percent— than White women since 1999. The National Bulosan Center compared women's earnings based on data from the last U.S. Decennial Census and its comparable 2006 U.S. Census American Community Survey. This finding is surprising because we would at least expect U.S. Filipinas to improve economically close to the same rate as White women, during the national economic boom since 2002. Nonetheless, U.S. Filipinas confront growing racial and gender problems in the arena of paid work.

These problems are amplified in particular local labor markets. In Hawai'i, the earnings growth rate for Filipinas is 50 percent less than White women. In areas such as Seattle, Washington and San Francisco-Oakland-San Jose, California, the earnings growth rates for Filipinas were closer to White women, at about five percent. While a five percent increase in the earning growth rate gap seems like an advance, the actual earnings gap between Filipinas and White women remains 15 percent. In northern California, this earning gap is about $9,700 annually.

In cities such as New York where there are highly skilled nurses and medical professionals working long hours, we would expect Filipinas to be doing well. The study reveals otherwise. In 1999, U.S. Filipinas living in New York City earned, on average, two thousand more than White women. In stark contrast in 2005, U.S. Filipinas in the city earned two thousand less than White women. As a result, the earning growth rate is 50 percent more for U.S. Filipinas in the city relative to White women.

On average, U.S. Filipinas have a **higher rate of formal labor force participation:** 65.5 percent for Filipinas compared to only 59.1 percent for the women in the general population. About 70 percent of U.S. Filipinas work in the for-profit sector (in hospitals, nursing care facilities, hotels/motels, eating establishments, and retail stores) while 10 percent work for nonprofits (such as nurses in health care organizations, accountants, and office assistants). Six percent of them work for local governments (such as elementary and middle school teachers), 4.3 percent for state governments, and 4.4 for the federal government (such as nurses in hospitals, for the postal service, for the U.S. navy or air force). Moreover, one percent of U.S. Filipinas own their own business. Over half of these women are physicians, surgeons, and dentists. The others run their own real estate or employment service companies.

Beyond earning disparities, Filipinas continue to face hardship in other areas of employment and social life in the U.S. Take for example the women healthcare workers—many of them working as nurses—who are currently involved in the legal battle against the Sentosa owners in

U.S. Filipinos work to advance women's interests.

the New York state court. These contract migrant workers were illegally recruited, are unwittingly trafficked from the Philippines to work in the U.S., and then accused by the New York State that the workers endangered their patients as they attempted to free themselves from forced servitude.

Then there is a single mother and her sons who were unwarrantedly tasered in an excessive manner and physically assaulted at a local park for seemingly no wrongdoing by the San Jose, California police in 2007. More than a year later, the Custodio family members are still in court to defend their innocence while ironically the police officers remain in duty.

And, there are thousands of invisible Filipinas in the U.S. experiencing intimate and interpersonal violence and emotional abuse at home and in their relationships. There are also U.S. Filipina lesbians who face public and familial violence and social and institutional exclusion due to their sexual identity and practices. For these Filipinas, there are relatively few safe spaces to share their experiences.

In general, U.S. Filipinas experience the combined assault of sexism, racial oppression, and economic exploitation. Sexism is the institutional patriarchal practice and belief that men are more worthy and superior to women, and therefore women deserve less economically, politically, and socially. Filipinas face economic insecurity, gender and sexual stereotyping, physical and mental health issues, and issues of domestic and interpersonal violence. Unequal gender relations, feudal famil-

U.S. Filipinas mobilize to stop human trafficking.

ial practices, and U.S. and Philippines economic factors structure these acts of interpersonal violence. Often time, this violence is deemed as normal to avoid further household and economic complications. Moreover Filipinas are increasingly becoming heads of household, further intensifying childcare and economic obligations. Migrant women tend to feel that they cannot leave their partner due to strong economic and emotional bonds.

Filipinas also face gendered violence, exploitation, sexual objectification, and racialized gender stereotyping. Some of them are victims of sexual assault and human trafficking. This objectification and gender oppression have roots in the sexist violence perpetrated by the historical and ongoing U.S. military presence in the Philippines. In addition, Spanish and U.S. colonization changed Filipino family and gender relations so that the nuclear heterosexual family and the male head of household as the main economic provider became the norm. As such, Filipinas were expected to be housewives to raise children. Over time, Filipinas were increasingly expected to contribute to the income of the family. This is one reason why many women seek employment outside of the Philippines. Moreover, U.S. immigration and family laws affect Filipina labor migration to the U.S. and promote increased economic and social hardship for U.S. Filipinas.

Tables 5, 8, 10, 29, and 31 provide further details on regional variations. More research is needed on family concerns for U.S. Filipinas—as such issues of divorce and conservative feudal values—and reproductive health and rights issues such as abortion.

The U.S. Filipino transgender and lesbian communities fighting for immigrant rights.

What are the social portrait and condition of U.S. Filipino lesbians, gay men, bisexual people, and transgender people?

There are about 400,000 U.S. Filipino lesbians, gay men, bisexuals, and transgender people (LGBT) who are potential targets of violence and social exclusion due to their sexual identities and expression. They face oppression from reactionary laws, ultra-religious beliefs, and systematic racism, sexism, heterosexism, "bi-phobia," and the institutional attempts to control their sexuality.

Initially they tend to face difficulty in "coming-out" to parents and family members. With greater political consciousness regarding sexual politics, they gain greater confidence on their sexual identity and wellbeing. Often in the Philippines, middle-class LGBTs—who tend to be in heterosexual marriages—fear publicly acknowledging their sexuality because it might negatively affect their family's social and economic standing. More working-class LGBTs tend to be open with family members and others in the community. The particularities of these issues in the U.S. need to be explored further.

Note that the term LGBT remains contentious, which can be viewed as homogenizing important differences among sexual minority groups' concrete conditions and distinct demands for social reform. At present, there is no broadly accepted term, due to personal preference, historical awareness, political affiliation, and organizing experience. Other possible terms include sexual minorities, the sexually oppressed, queers, and lesbian, gay, bisexual, transgender people, transsexual people, queers, and intersex people (LGBTTQI).

What are the social portrait and condition of U.S. Filipino youth and students?

There are about two million Filipino youth and students in the U.S. Fifty-one percent of them are female. Eighty-two percent of them have U.S. citizenship. Sixty-nine percent of them were born in the U.S. For

Table 27. U.S. Filipino Youth, By Census Regions

Age	USA		Los Angeles, Riverside, Orange Cnty CA		SF, SJ, Oakland, CA		Honolulu, HI region		NYC, N. NJ, Long Island, CT, PA	
	% Filipinos	% All	% Filipinos	% All	% Filipinos	% All	% Filipinos	% All	% Filipinos	% All
Under 5	8.1*	6.8	7.3	7.8	7.3*	6.4	8.9*	6.5	7.0*	6.8
Under 18	28.9*	25.7	26.9	28.5	27.2*	23.6	32.2*	23.8	24.8	24.8
18 to 24 years	11.0*	9.6	10.8*	10.0	10.6*	8.9	10.7*	10.1	9.7*	8.7
25 to 29 years	7.8*	6.9	7.5	7.7	7.7	7.9	7.6*	7.5	7.7*	7.0

Age	San Diego, CA region		Chicago, IL-Gary, IN-Kenosha, WI		Seattle, Tacoma, Bremerton, WA		Washington, DC-Baltimore, MD, VA, WV region		Las Vegas, NV, AZ region		Sacramento-Yolo, CA region	
	% Filipinos	% All	% Filipinos	% All	% Filipinos	% All	% Filipinos	% All	% Filipinos	% All	% Filipinos	% All
Under 5	7.8*	7.1	7.6*	7.4	8.6*	6.5	7.7*	6.8	8.7*	7.3	8.7*	6.9
Under 18	29.0*	25.7	25.2	26.9	31.3*	24.8	23.5*	25.3	29.2*	25.3	31.4*	27.1
18 to 24 years	11.7*	11.3	10.3*	9.5	11.6*	9.5	10.2*	8.7	10.7*	8.8	12.9*	9.7
25 to 29 years	7.6	7.9	9.3*	7.5	7.7*	7.4	8.2*	7.2	7.5	7.5	7.5*	6.7

Note: A "*" symbol indicates overrepresentation compared to the general population. Source: U.S. Census 2000 SF-4 (Tables DP-2 and P-1)

U.S. Filipino youth and students.

those born in the Philippines, over half of them came before 1996. For those Filipinos enrolled in school, 10.2 percent are in nursery school and kindergarten, 39.2 percent are in elementary, 20.6 percent are in high school, and 30 percent are in college or graduate schools. They typically experience racial profiling, police brutality, and lack economic opportunities. Moreover some are keen on learning more about Philippine issues and cultural heritage.

Among people 14 to 35 years old, 3.2 percent dropout from formal schooling;

Table 28. U.S. Filipino Students, By Census Regions

In School	USA		Los Angeles, Riverside, Orange Cnty CA		SF, SJ, Oakland, CA		Honolulu, HI region		NYC, N. NJ, Long Island, NY, CT, PA	
	% Filipinos	% All	% Filipinos	% All	% Filipinos	% All	% Filipinos	% All	% Filipinos	% All
Kindergarten, nursery, pre-k	10.0	11.9	9.0	11.0	9.5	11.1	10.7	10.7	10.6	12.7
Grade 1-8	39.7	43.9	37.9	43.9	38.5	39.5	46.0	40.7	38.3	42.6
Grade 9-12	19.9	21.4	18.6	21.0	19.4	19.5	22.5	20.6	18.1	21.0
College or graduate sch.	30.4*	22.8	34.4*	24.0	32.6*	29.5	20.8	28.0	33.0*	23.7

In School	San Diego, CA region		Chicago, IL-Gary, IN-Kenosha, WI		Seattle, Tacoma, Bremerton, WA		Washington, DC-Baltimore, MD, VA, WV region		Las Vegas, NV, AZ region		Sacramento-Yolo, CA region	
	% Filipinos	% All	% Filipinos	% All	% Filipinos	% All	% Filipinos	% All	% Filipinos	% All	% Filipinos	% All
Kindergarten, nursery, pre-k	8.7	10.8	9.4	13.2	10.6	11.7	9.9	12.1	9.9	11.9	7.9	10.6
Grade 1-8	38.6	40.7	34.6	43.8	39.8	43.4	38.3	42.7	43.6	48.3	40.4	42.1
Grade 9-12	20.4*	19.3	18.7	20.4	19.9*	21.3	19.7	20.3	22.7*	20.8	17.8	20.2
College or graduate sch.	32.3*	29.2	36.8*	22.6	27.2*	23.6	32.0*	24.9	23.7*	19.0	33.9*	27.0

Note: A "*" symbol indicates overrepresentation compared to the general population. Source: U.S. Census 2000 SF-4 (Table DP-2)

they were not enrolled in school and had not graduated from high school. Surprisingly, fifty-four percent of these out-of-school youth are born in the U.S. For U.S. Filipinos between ages 25 and 35 years, 96 percent had at least graduated from high school and 47 percent had a bachelor's degree or higher.

Seventy-four percent of students who are in school and 16 years and older are gainfully employed. The median age of these working students is 23. The median annual income for U.S. Filipino working students was $10,400 in 2005. They typically worked 35 weeks and for 30 hours per week annually. They are employed in occupations such as cashier (8.4 percent of working Filipinos), retail salespersons (7.1 percent), waiters and waitresses (4.1 percent), registered nurses (3.2 percent),

nursing, psychiatric, and home health aides (2.8 percent), and costumer service representatives (2.4 percent). Tables 5, 27, and 28 describe regional variations on the characteristics and issues of youth and students.

Some of the major student and campus issues pertaining to U.S. Filipinos that need further research include: (a) tuition and fee hikes and access to affordable education, (b) privatization of public education, (c) vocationalization of learning (i.e. trends in popular college majors and why), (d) curricular content such as regarding Philippine issues and U.S. Filipino issues, and Philippine languages, (e) student progress towards graduation (i.e. dropout), (f) differences in educational access and opportunities between Filipino migrants and Filipino descendants (i.e.

U.S. Filipino youth campaigning on racial profiling issues.

What are the social portrait and condition of U.S. Filipino seniors?

There are about 350,000 Filipino seniors—those 65 years and over—in the U.S., about 8.7 percent of U.S. Filipinos. Sixty-four percent of them have ages between 65 and 74. Most of them are women, about 59 percent Filipinas compared to 41 percent Filipino men. Over half of them live in California. Eighty nine percent were born in the Philippines; nevertheless 81 percent have U.S. citizenship. For those born in the Philippines, the median year of first entry into the U.S. was 1978. Thirty-seven have at least completed a bachelor college degree. The other 36 percent have at least received a high school diploma. Thirty five percent are still gainfully employed. The top three occupations for Filipino seniors are physician and surgeons (5.6 percent), maid and housekeeping (5.2 percent), and accountants and auditors (4.1 percent). The median total income was $12,000 even though when most of them worked full-time year round.

In addition, 67 percent receives Social Security retirement income, typically around $8,400 (in 2005). Twenty four percent receives non-social security retirement income, around about $10,350 (in 2005). Fourteen percent receives supplemental social security income, typically around $6,100 (in 2005). Less than one percent receives Social Security Supplemental Security Income (SSI), Aid to Family and Dependent Children (AFDC), and other social welfare income, typically

community college versus four-year state and private institutions), (g) recruitment in U.S. military, security agencies, and law enforcement, and (h) deepening our profile on working students.

Some of the major U.S. Filipino youth issues that need further research include: (a) relationship with parents and bridging the expectation gap, (b) the experiences of latch-key children who have parents working late or night shifts, (c) lifestyle practices and social activities (i.e. sports, video-games, shopping, and so on), (d) work experiences, economic, and social mobility, (e) bridging unity between migrant and descendant youth, (f) out-of-school youth issues, (g) sexuality, pregnancy, and relations concerns, (h) isolation, suicide, and mental health issues, (i) religion and spirituality, (j) sex work, (k) substance use and dealing, and (l) gangsterism and masculine violence.

around $1,500 in 2005. Table 5 provides additional details on regional variations.

Seniors depend on sons, daughters, and other immediate family members for financial resources, transportation, and attending to personal affairs. They face rising cost of healthcare and living, given their limited income. Their limited English proficiency restricts their access to community and social service resources. This dependency grows out of a sense of familiar obligation. They tend to watch over the grandchildren. They are uprooted from their strong ties in the Philippines. Many resent not being able to go back to the Philippines. They visit the Philippines to gain access to cheaper health care. They typically attend church, go grocery shopping, and take part of social and recreational activities with peers such as gambling, line dancing, and singing karaoke.

What is the social portrait and condition of Filipinos living with disability in U.S. society?

There are about 350,000 U.S. Filipinos living with some form of disability, which is about 8.9 percent of the overall Filipino population. Most disabilities are work related. Most of them are women (55 percent Filipinas). The median age is 60 years. The likelihood of having a disability varied by age—from three percent of people 5 to 15 years old, to 6.8 percent of people 16 to 64 years old, and to 40 percent of those 65 and older. Seventy six percent of U.S. Filipinos with disability were born in the Philippines. About eighty percent have U.S. citizenship. For those born in the Philippines, the median year of first entry into the U.S. was 1983. Twenty-seven have at least completed a bachelor college degree. The other 32 percent have at least received a high school diploma. About 31 percent are gainfully employed. The top occupations for them are registered nurses (4.5 percent), nursing and home health aides

(4.1 percent), cashiers (3.9 percent), maids and housekeeping cleaners (2.6 percent), personal and home care aides (2.4 percent), and store clerks and order fillers (2.4 percent). The median income was $19,200 even most of them worked full-time year round. Table 5 provides further details on regional variations.

Some disability issues pertaining to U.S. Filipinos that need further research include: (a) the prevalence of stigma, discrimination, family shame, and family acceptance, (b) access to social service resources including high cost of drug treatments, (c) the causes of disabilities, and (d) the rate of autism.

Bangsa Moros in the U.S. oppose the Philippine government's labor export policy.

What is the social portrait of Filipino religious groups in U.S. society?

U.S. Filipinos practice a range of religious faith and spirituality. Eighty percent of them are raised in Roman Catholic households. Eight percent are practicing Methodists, Episcopalians, and other Protestant denominations. About 2,700 religious workers are employed in various institutions. A few of them work in areas with a sizeable Filipino concentration, yet many others do not. Newly arrived workers with R-1 visas report increased scrutiny over their movement and employment by the U.S. Department of Homeland Security.

About three to six percent of U.S. Filipinos are Bangsa Moro such as Maguindanaos, Maranaos, and Tausogs. Particularly since September 11, 2001, many of them face threats, harm, profile, discrimination, and social exclusion because of their religious identification and practices. Various audiences often exoticize their cultural and religious practices and performances.

What is the social portrait of Philippine national minorities in U.S. society?

There are about 400,000 to 600,000 Philippine national and ethnic minorities in the U.S. such as the Igorots, Aetas, and Chinese Filipinos. In some areas, there are strong ethnic and cultural organizations. Various audiences often exoticize the cultural practices of indigenous performers from the Philippines, without a deep understanding of their ongoing land struggles, economic concerns, political rights, and cultural survival struggles. Further research on their social conditions is needed.

Table 29. U.S. Government and Nonprofit Employees, By Gender and Census Regions

Government & non-profit employees	USA		Los Angeles, Riverside, Orange Cnty CA		SF, SJ, Oakland, CA		Honolulu, HI region		NYC, N. NJ, Long Island, NY, CT, PA	
	% Filipinos	% All	% Filipinos	% All	% Filipinos	% All	% Filipinos	% All	% Filipinos	% All
In armed forces	1.3*	0.5	0.3*	0.2	0.2	0.2	1.3	5.6	0.1	0.1
Men										
Local gov't	4.9	5.6	6.8*	6.2	4.5	5.5	3.4	4.0	3.0	8.0
State gov't	3.5	3.7	2.3*	2.2	2.1	2.6	6.1	8.3	1.7	2.8
Federal gov't	6.6*	2.8	5.3*	1.9	4.1*	2.3	8.0	9.9	13.0*	2.4
Non-profit group	5.1*	4.4	5.0*	3.6	7.7*	4.2	3.2	5.1	8.8*	5.3
Women										
Local gov't	5.7	8.8	8.1	10.8	6.6	9.3	1.7	2.3	8.1	11.3
State gov't	4.7	5.9	3.4	4.2	3.1	4.0	9.0	14.3	3.4	3.9
Federal gov't	4.0*	2.6	2.6*	1.7	2.6*	2.1	5.1	6.3	2.6*	2.0
Non-profit group	9.7*	10.3	9.3*	7.4	14.2*	8.9	3.0	5.5	9.3*	11.2

Government & non-profit employees	San Diego, CA region		Chicago, IL-Gary, IN-Kenosha, WI		Seattle, Tacoma, Bremerton, WA		Washington, DC-Baltimore, MD, VA, WV region		Las Vegas, NV, AZ region		Sacramento-Yolo, CA region	
	% Filipinos	% All	% Filipinos	% All	% Filipinos	% All	% Filipinos	% All	% Filipinos	% All	% Filipinos	% All
In armed forces	4.7*	4.0	0.6*	0.2	2.6*	1.5	1.6*	1.1	0.7*	0.6	0.2	0.2
Men												
Local gov't	5.5	5.5	3.5	5.9	5.2*	4.9	3.1	5.4	3.3	5.2	5.4	5.5
State gov't	3.4*	3.1	1.7	1.8	2.7	4.8	1.7	2.8	0.7	1.7	12.5*	9.5
Federal gov't	15.9*	5.6	4.0*	2.0	6.9*	3.8	13.0*	11.9	3.4*	2.2	5.3*	2.9
Non-profit group	3.5	3.9	7.7*	5.0	3.9	4.2	8.8*	6.2	1.7*	1.6	3.6	4.0
Women												
Local gov't	7.5	9.6	4.8	8.5	2.8	7.1	2.6	9.6	4.6	8.6	5.8	10.2
State gov't	3.6	4.8	2.9	3.1	2.0	8.6	2.2	3.8	1.5	2.9	16.6*	14.1
Federal gov't	7.7*	3.6	3.5*	2.1	10.7*	2.9	9.0	11.7	1.4	1.9	2.7*	2.0
Non-profit group	2.5	7.8	3.0	3.9	12.0*	9.8	5.4	4.8	2.8	4.1	6.6	6.6

Note: A "*" symbol indicates overrepresentation compared to the general population. Source: U.S. 2000 Census SF-4 (Table QT-P25)

U.S. Filipino government and nonprofit workers and professionals.

What is the social portrait of U.S. Filipino government workers and professionals?

There are around 586,000 U.S. Filipinos employed as U.S. government workers and professionals. Nationally, they tend to be overrepresented in federal government jobs such as postal carriers. Filipinas tend to be in local government jobs compared to state and federal government jobs. Most of these government jobs tend to be secured and unionized. Moreover, they do

Table 30. U.S. Filipino Veterans of the U.S. Military, By Period of Service and Census Regions

	USA		Los Angeles, Riverside, Orange Cnty CA		SF, SJ, Oakland, CA		Honolulu, HI region		NYC, N. NJ, Long Island, NY, CT, PA	
	% Filipinos	% All	% Filipinos	% All	% Filipinos	% All	% Filipinos	% All	% Filipinos	% All
U.S. veterans	7.0	12.7	5.6	9.0	6.6	9.8	8.1	14.0	2.5	8.6
Period of service										
WWII	12.8	21.7	20.1	23.0	15.8	22.8	12.0	18.7	23.1	27.6
Korean War	7.5	15.3	7.4	15.7	7.5	15.3	12.3	15.1	8.3	16.6
Vietnam War	34.4*	31.7	28.5	30.6	33.8*	33.1	35.1*	33.2	20.6	26.7
1st Persian Gulf War	27.2*	11.5	23.9*	10.2	20.0*	8.8	20.2*	18.5	21.8*	6.4

	San Diego, CA region		Chicago, IL-Gary, IN-Kenosha, WI		Seattle, Tacoma, Bremerton, WA		Washington, DC-Baltimore, MD, VA, WV region		Las Vegas, NV, AZ region		Sacramento-Yolo, CA region	
	% Filipinos	% All	% Filipinos	% All	% Filipinos	% All	% Filipinos	% All	% Filipinos	% All	% Filipinos	% All
U.S. veterans	13.6	14.6	3.1	9.8	9.7	15.4	7.3	13.2	7.5	16.3	9.2	13.7
Period of service												
WWII	8.4	20.2	17.3	22.9	8.3	16.9	8.3	16.9	9.8	19.3	18.0	21.0
Korean War	9.2	15.6	4.5	14.1	5.6	13.2	5.6	13.2	10.0	17.8	6.7	16.3
Vietnam War	44.2*	34.0	32.3*	29.9	37.8*	34.8	37.8*	34.8	39.1*	33.2	34.1*	35.5
1st Persian Gulf War	34.4*	20.1	30.5*	9.3	35.2*	17.0	35.2*	17.0	23.9*	12.1	20.9*	10.1

Note: A "*" symbol indicates overrepresentation compared to the general population. Source: U.S. Census 2000 SF-4

not hold senior positions in government, nor assert major influence in policy. In effect, there exists a glass ceiling for U.S. Filipinos attempting to advance in public service. Table 29 provides further details on regional variations.

There are a few U.S. Filipinos employed by the Philippine government in its consulate and missions located in certain U.S. cities. The positions range from the ambassador, consult general, lawyers, clerks, trade mission representatives, domestic workers, and cooks.

More research is needed on U.S. Filipinos working in government jobs.

What is the social portrait and condition of Filipino military personnel and war veterans in U.S. society?

ACTIVE U.S. MILITARY PERSONNEL There are about 15,000 Filipinos working for the U.S. Armed Forces, about 0.5 percent of U.S. Filipinos. Fifty-six percent of them work as support staff and are not engaged in frontline military operations. Twenty-eight percent are soldiers and 13 percent are enlisted military officers: they are serving in active duty for the post-2001 wars. Thirty eight percent of Filipino military personnel are in the U.S. Navy, 22 percent in the U.S. Air Force, 19 percent in the U.S. Army, 5 percent in the U.S. Marines, and the remaining ones serve in other capaci-

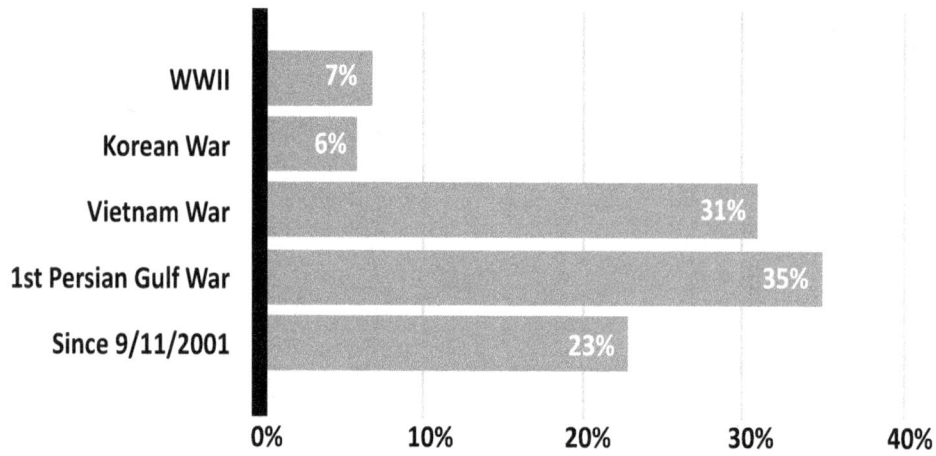

Figure 23. Period of Service for Filipinos Veterans of U.S. Wars. Source: U.S. Census American Community Survey 2006.

ties in the U.S. Armed Forces. Table 29 provides further details on regional variations.

Most of the active military personnel are men (81 percent). The median age is 32. About 58 percent were born in the Philippines; yet ten percent do not have U.S. citizenship. For those born in the Philippines, the median year of first entry into the U.S. was 1987. Only twenty-four percent have at least completed a bachelor college degree. Thirty five percent are still gainfully employed. The median annual income was $35,000 in 2005.

Children are affected growing up in military families. Some face more intense forms of feudal relations from the military father, hardship due to separating from the military parent due to deployment, and hardship due to greater geographic dislocation.

U.S. WAR VETERANS There are about 121,000 Filipino veterans living that served in U.S. wars and military interventions, about three percent of U.S. Filipinos.

About 25 percent of all Filipino veterans have been in active duty during or after September 2001; 35 percent served in active duty from August 1999 to August 2001; 31 percent from September 1980 to July 1990; 22 percent from May 1975 to July 1980; 31 percent from August 1964 to April 1975 (Vietnam War period); 12 percent from February 1955 to July 1964; six percent from July 1950 to January 1955 (Korean War period); one percent from January 1947 to June 1950; and seven percent from December 1941 to December 1946 (World War Two).

Most Filipino veterans are men (88 percent). The median age is 53. About 65 percent were born in the Philippines; yet as U.S. veterans, 4.4 percent still do not have U.S. citizenship. For those born in the Philippines, the median year of first entry into the U.S. was 1974. About 51 percent reside in California: 12 percent in Hawai'i, 4 percent in Florida, and 3 percent in Nevada. Only twenty-five percent have at least completed a bachelor college degree.

Table 31. U.S. Filipino Unemployed and Unpaid Family Workers, By U.S. Census Regions

	USA		Los Angeles, Riverside, Orange Cnty CA		SF, SJ, Oakland, CA		NYC, N. NJ, Long Island, NY, CT, PA		Honolulu, HI region	
	% Filipinos	% All	% Filipinos	% All	% Filipinos	% All	% Filipinos	% All	% Filipinos	% All
Unemployed	5.5	5.8	5.9	7.4	4.5	4.5	4.4	6.7	6.8*	6.2
Unpaid Family Worker										
Men	0.2	0.3	0.2	0.3	0.2	0.2	0.1	0.2	0.1	0.3
Women	0.3	0.4	0.3	0.5	0.1	0.4	0.3	0.3	0.4	0.4

	San Diego, CA region		Chicago, IL-Gary, IN-Kenosha, WI		Seattle, Tacoma, Bremerton, WA		Washington, DC-Baltimore, MD, VA, WV region		Las Vegas, NV, AZ region		Sacramento-Yolo, CA region	
	% Filipinos	% All	% Filipinos	% All	% Filipinos	% All	% Filipinos	% All	% Filipinos	% All	% Filipinos	% All
Unemployed	5.6*	3.6	3.5	6.3	5.7*	5.1	3.3	4.5	7.4*	6.6	6.8*	6.2
Unpaid Family Worker												
Men	0.2	0.2	0.1	0.2	0.2	0.2	0.1	0.1	0.1	2.2	0.2	0.2
Women	0.2	0.4	0.1	0.3	0.1	0.3	0.2	0.2	0.3	0.3	0.1	0.3

Note: A "*" symbol indicates overrepresentation compared to the general population. Source: U.S. Census 2000 SF-4 (Table DP3 & QT-P25)

The top three occupations for Filipino veterans are postal office clerks (3.5 percent), registered nurses (2.5 percent), miscellaneous managers (2.4 percent), hand laborers and freight, stock and material movers (2.3 percent), and private security guards (2.1 percent). Their median annual income was $38,050 in 2005. The top three occupations for veterans with active duty since September 2001 are registered nurses (3.8 percent), clinical laboratory technicians (3.3 percent), aircraft mechanics and service technicians (3.3 percent), and store clerks and order fillers (3.3 percent). Their median annual income was $30,000 in 2005. Table 30 provides further details on period of service and regional variations.

More research is needed on U.S. Filipino military personnel and war veteran issues such as (1) war bride families, (2) the relationship of migration and U.S. Navy deployment, (3) mail order brides and U.S. military families, and (4) forced conscription for some with options of going to jail or serving the military.

What is the social portrait of Filipino politicians in the U.S.?

A number of former and current U.S. Filipino politicians have longstanding working relationship with the Philippine consulate and missions located in U.S. cities. They also work closely with several Republican and Democratic party-machineries across the U.S., leading national and regional politicians in the Philippines, and with senior staff and officers of organizations such as the National Federation of Filipino American Associations. Some influential politicians have inconsistent records in supporting grassroots U.S. Filipino organizations that serve working families and marginalized communities. More research is needed on Filipino politicians in the U.S.

Table 32. U.S. Filipinos Residing in State-Funded Institutions[1], By U.S. Census Regions

	Percent of Filipinos	Percent of General Pop.
Census-Defined Regions		
Honolulu, HI region	0.5	0.7
Los Angeles, Riverside, Orange county CA region	0.3	0.9
San Francisco, San Jose, Oakland, CA region	0.3	1.0
Sacramento-Yolo, CA region	0.3	1.0
Chicago, IL-Gary, IN-Kenosha, WI region	0.3	0.8
Seattle, Tacoma, Bremerton, WA region	0.2	0.8
Las Vegas, NV-AZ region	0.2	0.8
San Diego, CA region	0.2	0.9
NY, North NJ, Long Island, NY region	0.1	1.1
Washington, DC, Baltimore, MD-VA-WV region	0.1	1.1
U.S.A.	*0.3*	*1.4*

Note: (1) These institutions include prisons, jails, group homes and similar places. Source: U.S. Census 2000 SF-2 (Table DP-1)

What is the social portrait of non-traditional earners among U.S. Filipinos?

About 200,000 to 320,000 U.S. Filipinos are non-traditional earners and part of the informal underground economy. This group is composed of irregular workers, internationally trafficked people, casual household helpers, small store helpers, peddlers, restaurant helpers, day laborers, and certain parts of unauthorized migrants. Generally, they do not have any regular source of earning and little or no means of consistent livelihood. Tables 31 profiles U.S. Filipinos who are unemployed and unpaid. Further research is needed on non-traditional earners.

What is the social portrait of U.S. Filipinos living in the margins of society?

There are about 120,000 to 160,000 Filipinos who are living in the margins of U.S. society and part of the informal underground economy. They experience forced idleness, as they are not easily absorbed in the economy. They engage in "get rich quick" schemes and loan shark and insurance scams as well as con-artist, anti-social, and illegal activities. Some are prone to acts of physical violence. Some of them become entangled within the law enforcement system (see Table 32). Further research is needed on Filipinos living in the margins of U.S. society.

Afterword

All told, the dismal conditions of oppression and exploitation of U.S. Filipinos have been aggravated and deepened by the so-called policies of export-oriented Philippine economy and "free market" globalization and by unjust schemes of U.S. and Philippine governments to use state terrorism to suppress the widespread social discontent and resistance of the people.

All export products of the Philippines are in a state of depression. The Philippine government is extremely dependent on the foreign exchange remittances of overseas Filipinos and is ever more extortionate in its exactions. And worse, it emboldens foreign governments and employers to subject Filipino compatriots to the most exploitative conditions of employment.

More than ever, National Alliance for Filipino Concerns (NAFCON) members must strengthen themselves by upholding, defending, and advancing rights of U.S. Filipinos. For this purpose, NAFCON members must engage in study, hold educational gatherings, disseminate crucial facts and information, build chapters among Filipinos and their families, and mobilize them in conjunction with the Filipino people everywhere in the movement for national freedom and democracy in the Philippines.

The crisis of the world economic system is daily worsening and inflicting more and more acute suffering on working people. It is of urgent necessity that NAFCON members consolidate and expand their ranks in order to cope with the growing economic, social and political problems, meet the challenges in defending the rights and interests of U.S. Filipinos and their families, and aim for a better future for them and other struggling communities.

References

Critical Filipina and Filipino Studies Collective (CFFSC). 2004. *Resisting Homeland Security: Organizing Against Unjust Removals of U.S. Filipinos*. San Jose, CA: Critical Filipina and Filipino Studies Collective.

IBON. 2004. *Philippine History and Government*. Quezon City, Philippines: IBON Books.

Migrante International. 1996. *The LEP Primer*. Quezon City, Philippines: Migrante International.

U.S. Census Bureau. 2003a. *U.S. Census of Population and Housing: Census 2000 Summary File 2*. Washington, DC: U.S. Census Bureau.

————. 2003b. *U.S. Census of Population and Housing: Census 2000 Summary File 4*. Washington, DC: U.S. Census Bureau.

————. 2006. *American Community Survey 2005*. Washington, DC: U.S. Census Bureau.

————. 2007. *American Community Survey 2006*. Washington, DC: U.S. Census Bureau.

————. 2008. American Community Survey 2007. Washington, DC: U.S. Census Bureau.

U.S. Department of Homeland Security. 2003. *2003 Yearbook of Immigration Statistics*. Washington, DC: U.S. Department of Homeland Security.

————. 2004. *2004 Yearbook of Immigration Statistics*. Washington, DC: U.S. Department of Homeland Security.

————. 2006. *2006 Yearbook of Immigration Statistics*. Washington, DC: U.S. Department of Homeland Security.